MOM ALWAYS SAID, "DON'T PLAY BALL IN THE HOUSE"

(And Other Stuff We Learned from TV)

MOM ALWAYS SAID, "DON'T PLAY BALL IN THE HOUSE"
(And Other Stuff We Learned from TV)

David and Joe Borgenicht

CHILTON BOOK COMPANY
RADNOR, PENNSYLVANIA

Copyright©1996 by David and Joe Borgenicht

All Rights Reserved
Published in Radnor, Pennsylvania 19089, by Chilton Book Company

No part of this book may be reproduced, transmitted, or stored,
in any form or by any means, electronic or mechanical, without prior written permission from the publisher.

Designed and Produced by March Tenth, Inc.
Cover design by Harry Choron

Manufactured in the United States of America
Library of Congress Cataloging-in-Publication Data

Mom always said, "Don't play ball in the house," and other stuff
we learned from TV / [compiled by] by David and Joe Borgenicht.
p. cm.
Includes index.
ISBN 0-8019-8771-7 (pb)
1. Television programs—United States—Quotations, maxims, etc.
I. Borgenicht, David. II. Borgenicht, Joe.
PN1992.58.M66 1996
791.45'75'0973—dc20   96-19056
                                                                          CIP

2 3 4 5 6 7 8 9 0   5 4 3 2 1 0 9 8 7

*T*o all our best friends and sidekicks: Jennie Picolo, Robin, and Jason Novak. To all our pets: Tiger, Lassie, Flipper, Pappy Shakes, Shmoey, Sato, Harpo, and Kitty Cohen. To all our wives and girlfriends: Mary Beth (wah-wah-wah), Ms. Piggy, Shirley Feeney, Mrs. Roper, Melanie Koerpel, and Suzanne Simons.To all our hangouts: the Peach Pit, Al's, the Regal Beagle, South Street Souvlaki, and the Twilite Lounge. To all our fathers: Howard Cunningham, Ward Cleaver, Merrill Stubing, and Louis Borgenicht. And to all our mothers: Carol Brady, Abby Bradford, Shirley Partridge, and Nancy Borgenicht.

CONTENTS

*W*hen I first realized how good bad TV really was, I was watching *Three's Company*. It ran at 4:30 PM every day after school (wasn't I lucky?), and because my parents didn't get home until around 5:30 PM I could sneak a little TV with my brother before they got home. I did this every day religiously. And, eventually, I noticed something strange. I noticed that they only used two or three different plots. For example:

Plot One: Someone mishears something someone else was saying and takes it the wrong way. This causes much havoc, until the farcical final scene, in which everyone discovers the truth and makes up.

Plot Two: Through poor communication, all three roommates end up having a guest stay over. This causes much havoc, until the farcical final scene, in which everyone discovers the truth and makes up.

Plot Three: Larry has some hot date planned for him and Jack. Mr. Roper/Mr. Furley overhears this plan and decides to kick Jack out because he isn't gay. Jack again has to convince Mr. Roper/Mr. Furley that truly he *is* gay. This causes much havoc, until the farcical final scene, in which all is resolved and they all make up.

In time, I came to see that this formulaic approach was also true of my other favorite shows.

Gilligan's Island—How would they almost get off the island this time?

Love Boat—How would the loving pseudo-famous couples break up, them make up this week?

Bewitched—What would Endora do to mess up Durwood's ad campaign? Life was full of surprises and the unexpected. Except when it came to TV. I could count on TV. I could count on the Fonz. I could count on Lenny and Squiggy. I could count on Mr. Roarke. This I came to see, after hundreds of hours of covert TV watching. Ultimately, the TV characters became my sages. The shows became my Bibles. Their lines and catchphrases became my wisdom, their actions became my lessons, their mutterings my mantras. May they be yours as well.

PREFACE
by Joe Borgenicht

hy didn't I listen to my parents when they told me I could only watch one hour of TV a week? Why did I learn that if my brother and I took the *TV Guide* off the top of the TV, it wouldn't get warm while our parents were out on the town? Why did we watch as much as we did? It's a mad device. And it took me in. When I was twelve, my dog Pappy Shakes hung himself during the episode of *Gilligan's Island* in which the crew all escaped to the mad scientist's island and changed brains. I heard a loud bang outside just as Gilligan became Mary Anne, and I ignored it. That show cost me my dog's life. And still, I continued to watch. I can only think it's because there's something to talk about with friends the next day. The "did you see" approach is always a good way to fill an uncomfortable silence.

Actually, I don't think this way. I hate TV, even though it pays most of my bills. I was working on a film set some months ago. It was a TV movie produced by Wayne Rogers. One day a fight broke out between two strangers on the set. Wayne stepped in to break it up. As he was holding one of the fighters back, the breathless puncher looked up at him. "Sorry, Trapper," he said. I wouldn't have missed it for all the episodes of *M*A*S*H*. Television *is*. It will, barring the Apocalypse, never *not* be. It can be like a hot shower after a long hard workday. It can be a double bacon cheeseburger that you probably shouldn't have. But mostly it's a way to hang out with friends without really talking to them. This book is to us what the Bible was to the early Judeo-Christians. Here's the new mythology. Maybe we should just bury this book in the desert of Arizona so that in a few hundred years there will be churches filled with Charlie's Angels, Gilligan's Islams, and Brotherhood Brady's. It couldn't hurt.

ACKNOWLEDGMENTS

*N*o man is a *Gilligan's Island,* as the saying goes, and this book could not have been written without the help, cooperation, and acquiescence of many people, places, and things.

JOE'S LIST

Thanks to the Museum of Television and Radio in New York for their archives and collections. If you can't find a show on syndication or cable, the museum has it. When they don't, they are just as disappointed as you. Thanks to Lucy's Bar at St. Mark's and A, and to Lucy and Marco, because without them I'd still be TV buzzed. Thanks to my brother for seeing the Big Picture, the Big Idea, and the Big Kahuna episode of *Gidget;* and to my parents for only letting us watch an hour of TV a week. If it weren't for that rule, which needed to be broken, we probably would have never watched as much as we did. Thanks to all those choked pool shots and workplace mistakes punctuated with a heartfelt "D'o!" and, finally, to Ivy Pete and the Limbomaniacs, because they know when to turn off the TV. Thanks.

DAVE'S LIST

Thanks to everyone who helped us remember the highly significant content of these classic shows—in particular Virginia Mattingly, Ceri Jones, Brian Perrin, and anyone else I've forgotten. Thanks to the keepers of vast internet TV archives that I visited and borrowed from. I hope that in some small way, we have given as much to you as you have given to us. And I hope you always have too much free time. Thanks to our valiant editor, Troy Vozella, our designers, Sandy and Harry Choron, to Jeff Day, to Bruce McKenzie, and to Cathy Trefz for believing in the book even when no one else did, and for "Making Our Dreams Come True." Thanks to David Smith for understanding what ZOINKS! meant, and for taking on this project. A huge thanks to Suzanne Simons Borgenicht for enduring the insanity while Joe and I tortured ourselves by watching hours of television while researching this book. I love you even more than *I Love Lucy.* And most of all, thanks to my brother for keeping me from taking this (and other things) too seriously, and of course, for keeping me on intimate terms with this prairie.

INTRODUCTION

"*H*ome to me . . . is a shared electronic dream of cartoon memories, half-hour sit-coms, and national tragedies."

Douglas Coupland

Welcome home.

This book grew out of a phenomenon with which those born after 1960 are very well acquainted—a miracle that sits calmly in our living rooms, staring blankly at us as we stare blankly at it.

You know it well—television. Television has affected us in vast and untold ways, ways we may not fully understand for many years to come.

TV has become a common frame of reference for those of us who grew up in front of it—those of us who thought that the TV was not a household appliance but rather our third, somewhat less-demanding, parent. TV has replaced literature and mythology as the source of our generational canon. And TV references have become our common ground—a common base of knowledge that everyone who has ever watched TV can relate to.

Now more than ever we use this knowledge to express ourselves. TV words and moments are more than fond memories—they are ways to connect and relate to each other, to clarify points and make inside jokes, and to epitomize situations.

Every age has its allusions and mythology. Shakespeare had Milton. Milton had the Greeks. We have the Bradys. Instead of Dante and Hermes, we have Laverne and Shirley.

Like the Baby Boomers who can tell you exactly where they were when Kennedy was assassinated, we can tell you exactly where we were when the Challenger blew up (Journalism—4th period), or what words began *Fantasy Island* ("Dee plane! Dee plane!"), or hum the theme from *I Dream of Jeannie* ("Duuuh-dah! Dah dah dah-dah dah!"). Anyone born after 1960 can tell you exactly where he was when he had his "Darrincident"—the moment he realized that Dick Sargent had replaced Dick York on *Bewitched* (Joey and I were ten and eight years old, respectively), or who played Alice on *The Brady Bunch* ("And starring Ann B. Davis as Alice"), or whether he liked Jo or Blair better on *The Facts of Life*. (No contest, Jo.) And any self-respecting twentysomething can tell you exactly how she felt when she first learned that the darling of the seven seas—Julie McCoy, cruise director—had a drug problem.

My brother Joe and I set out to truly capture this phenomenon in *Mom Always Said, "Don't Play Ball in the House."* And we think we've done it.

Mom Always Said, "Don't Play Ball in the House" is an interactive guide to the TV shows we all grew up with—quotations, sayings, catch phrases, and songs that resonate to those of us shaped in front of the television. With more than 500 quotes, the lyrics to our favorite theme songs, *Schoolhouse Rock* songs, and dozens of entertaining extras—things like how to do the Laverne and Shirley dance, how to greet people like they did on the *Love Boat,* how to jump in a car like the Dukes of Hazzard, and how to win a fight like Captain Kirk—this is more than another book of TV trivia. It truly brings TV to life.

What's the impact of all this? Will it bring us closer to each other, forming Marshall McLuhan's Global Community? Will it destroy our culture, as Gerry Mander (his real name) suggested in *Four Arguments for the Elimination of Television?* Will there come a point in high school English that our kids will watch *MacGyver* instead of reading *Macbeth?*

Hell if we know. We just watched the damned stuff. We'll leave it for you to decide how it affected us.

So read, watch, and remember.

MOM ALWAYS SAID, "DON'T PLAY BALL IN THE HOUSE"

(And Other Stuff We Learned from TV)

WHAT YOU ARE ABOUT TO SEE IS REAL: OPENING WORDS

We remember beginnings the best.

This is not only because of sheer repetition, but also because openings are constructed to be memorable. We're meant to remember theme songs, opening narrations, commercial jingles, and classic opening lines better than any other part of the media canon.

The beginnings are memorable because, like a Greek chorus foreshadowing the action, like an overture for a Broadway musical, like the smell of a Pop Tart wafting through the house, the beginnings tantalize us, and lure us into their world with anticipation.

Within this chapter are the words, lyrics, and moments that began it all. It's like going home again.

● ● ● ● ● ● ● ● ● ● ● ● ● ● ● ● ●

"What you are about to see is real. The litigants on the screen are not actors. They are genuine citizens who, having filed their claims in a real small claims court, have been persuaded to drop their suits there and have them settled here, in this forum—*The People's Court.*"
Doug Lewellyn, *The People's Court*

"Welcome to Fantasy Island."
Mr. Roarke, *Fantasy Island*

"Once upon a time there were three little girls who went to the police academy. And they were assigned very hazardous duties. But I took them away from all that. . . . Uh . . . my name's Charlie."

Charlie, *Charlie's Angels*

"Good morning Mr. Phelps. The man you are looking at is General Ernesto Neram, the former dictator of Soora Niaca, who now lives in exile in his closely guarded Miami estate. In order to finance a military coup, which will return him to power, Neram is about to conclude a deal with this man, Frank Latham, a top syndicate leader. In exchange for several million dollars, Neram has agreed to legalize gambling in Soora Niaca and give all rights to the syndicate. Your mission, Jim, should you decide to accept it, is to stop Neram and the syndicate. As always, should you or any of your IM force be caught or killed, the Secretary will disavow any knowledge of your actions. This tape will self- destruct in five seconds. Good luck, Jim."

Opening Tape, *Mission: Impossible*

"There are those who believe that life here began out there, far across the universe, with tribes of humans who may have been the forefathers of the Egyptians, or the Toltecs, or the Mayans. They may have been the architects of the great pyramids, or the lost civilizations of Lemuria or Atlantis. Some believe that there may yet be brothers of man who even now fight to survive far, far away, amongst the stars."

Voice Over, *Battlestar Galactica*

"Space—the final frontier. These are the voyages of the Starship Enterprise. Our five-year mission: to explore strange, new worlds, to seek out new life and new civilizations, to boldly go where no man has gone before."

Captain Kirk, *Star Trek*

"Space—the final frontier. These are the voyages of the Starship Enterprise. Its continuing mission: to explore strange new worlds, to seek out new life and new civilizations, to boldly go where no one has gone before."

Captain Picard, *Star Trek: The Next Generation*

"In the year 1987, NASA launched the last of America's deep space probes. Aboard this compact starship a lone astronaut, Captain William Buck Rogers, was to experience cosmic forces beyond all comprehension. In a freak mishap, his life support systems were frozen by temperatures beyond imagination. Ranger 3 was blown out of its planned trajectory into an orbit a thousand times more vast: an orbit which was to return Buck Rogers to Earth five hundred years later."

Voice Over, *Buck Rogers in the 25th Century*

Great Phone Messages from Jim Rockford's Machine on THE ROCKFORD FILES

1. BEEP! Jimmy, it's Angel. Don't pay no attention to my other message. You're out of it. You're clean, no trouble at all. Just ignore the first message.

2. BEEP! Hi, Jim. Thanks for the dinner invitation. I'd love to, but does it have to be the taco stand?

3. BEEP! It's Jack. The check is in the mail. Sorry it's two years late. Sorry I misfigured my checking account and I'm overdrawn. Sorry I stopped payment on it. So, when it comes, tear it up. Sorry.

4. BEEP! It's Shirley at the Planted Pot. There's just no easy way to tell you this, Jim. We did everything we could. Your fern died.

5. BEEP! Jimmy, old buddy, buddy. It's Angel! You know how they allow you one phone call? Well, this is it.

6. BEEP! Hey, I saw your ad in the classified. Three African goats for sale. I keep calling and all I get is a machine. Is that a typo in the paper, or what?

7. BEEP! Hey, am I too late for those African goats? Haven't got the whole three hundred cash, but, like I've got a whole lot of homemade cheese. Maybe we could work something out.

8. BEEP! Jim, I have finally finished twelve long years of pyschotherapy and I'm now able to tell you just what I think of you. Would you please call me?

9. BEEP! That number forty you just picked up from Angelo's Pizza? Some scouring powder fell in there. Don't eat it. Hey, I hope you try your phone machine before dinner.

"Alpha Control's final analysis on the Jupiter 2's flight indicates, unhappily, that the space ship has either been destroyed, or must be presumed, *Lost in Space!*"
Voice Over, *Lost in Space*

"They arrived in fifty mother ships, offering their friendship and advance technology to Earth. . . . Skeptical of the Visitors, Mike Donovan and Juliet Parrish infiltrated their ranks . . . and

Steve Austin and NASA Dialogue

NASA: It looks good at NASA One.

Steve: Roger.

NASA: BCS Arm switch is on.

Steve: Okay, Victor.

NASA: Lining Rocket Arm switch is on.

Steve: Here comes the throttle.

NASA: Circuit breaker's in.

Steve: We have separation.

NASA: Roger.

Steve: In port and out ports are on.

NASA: Come in forward with the slide stick.

Steve: Looks good.

NASA: Ah, roger.

Steve: I've got a blowout in damper three!

NASA: Get your pitch to zero.

Steve: Pitch is out! I can't hold altitude!

NASA: Direction Alpha Hold is off . . . turn selectors . . . emergency!

Steve: Flight Com! I can't hold it! She's breaking up, she's break—

Narrator: Steve Austin. Astronaut. A man barely alive.

Oscar Goldman: Gentlemen, we can rebuild him. We have the technology. We have the capability to make the world's first bionic man. Steve Austin will be that man. Better than he was before. Better . . . stronger . . . faster.

soon discovered some startling secrets ('They're shipping food!'). The Resistance is all that stands between us . . . and the Visitors. . . ."

Voice Over, *V*

"Banded together from remote galaxies are thirteen of the most sinister villains of all time: the Legion of Doom! Dedicated to a single objective: the conquest of the universe! Only one group dares to challange this intergalactic bunch: the Superfriends. The Justice League of America vs. The Legion of Doom. This is the Challenge of the Superfriends."

Voice Over, *Superfriends*

"Heeeeyyyyy Yooooouuuu Guuuuuuyyyyssss!"

Rita Moreno, *Electric Company*

"It's . . . "

Old Hermit, *Monty Python's Flying Circus*

"And now for something completely different."

Newscaster, *Monty Python's Flying Circus*

"This is the city. Los Angeles, California. I work here. I carry a badge. It was Thursday, May 13, and it was cool in Los Angeles. We were working out of Detective Headquarters, Missing Persons section. The boss is Captain Diddian. My partner's Bill Gannon. My name's Friday. The story you are about to see is true. The names have been changed to protect the innocent."

Sergeant Joe Friday,
Dragnet

"Live from New York, it's Saturday Night!"

Saturday Night Live

The Make Your Own
MISSION: IMPOSSIBLE
Opening Tape

Let's face it, we've all got a few tasks we'd like the *Mission: Impossible* team to take care of for us. Now you can pretend you've hired the task force to do just that. Simply fill in the blanks with the required words and your mission is clear. These instructions will self-destruct in five seconds.

"Good morning, *(your name)*. A *(profession)*, *(second name)*, will arrive in *(name of a town)* via *(type of transportation)* on Friday. *(Second name)* has a *(event)* with the most powerful *(type of leadership position)* in this part of *(country)*, a man we know only by his *(noun)*, *(nickname)*. *(Second name's)* mission is to *(verb)* someone. We do not know whom he will *(same verb)*, or where, when, or how he will do it. We know that he will be wearing a *(adjective)* *(article of clothing)* and carrying a *(adjective)* *(noun)*. Your mission, should you choose to accept it, is to *(verb)* the *(event)* and discover the *(characteristic)* of *(nickname)*. This tape will *(verb)* in five seconds. *(Farewell expression)*, *(your name)*."

HENRY: When we first moved to New York we had a great apartment. Dirt cheap.

KIP: And we found out why it was so cheap.

HENRY: Our friend Amy said there was a great apartment in her building. Dirt Cheap.

KIP: But it's a hotel for women. OK. We made one adjustment.

HENRY: Now these ladies know us as Buffy and Hildegarde.

KIP: But they also know us as Kip and Henry, Buffy and Hildy's brothers.

HENRY: I am crazy about the blonde.

KIP: This experience is going to make a great book.

HENRY: See? It's all perfectly normal.

Bosom Buddies

"Tonight, on this stage, eight of the best new stars of 1984 will win $100,000 each. It's the exciting final round of competition on . . . *Star Search.*"
Ed McMahon,
Star Search

"Come on down! You're the next contestant on *The Price Is Right!*"
Johnny Olson,
The Price Is Right

"From Television City in Hollywood, California—this is *The $100,00 Pyramid!* Tonight, your guest stars are George Gobel and Audrey Landers. And now your host, Dick Clark!"
Announcer, *The $100,000 Pyramid*

"Good evening. I'm Chevy Chase, and you're not."
Chevy Chase, *"Weekend Update," (Saturday Night Live)*

"Faster than a rolling O. Stronger than silent E. Able to leap capital T in a single bound. Its a word. It's a plan. It's . . . Letterman!"
Voice Over, *Electric Company*

"Faster than a speeding bullet. More powerful than a locomotive. Able to leap tall buildings in a single bound. Look, up in the sky! It's a bird. It's a plane. It's Superman! Yes, it's Superman. Strange visitor from another planet who came to Earth with powers and abilities far beyond those of mortal men. Superman! Who can change the course of mighty rivers, bend steel in his bare hands. And who, disguised as Clark Kent, mild-mannered reporter for a great metropolitan newspaper, fights a never-ending battle for Truth, Justice, and the American Way. And now, another exciting episode in *The Adventures of Superman!*"
Voice Over, *The Adventures of Superman*

How to Do the LAVERNE AND SHIRLEY Dance

From 1976–1983 we were charmed all the way from Milwaukee to Los Angeles by two remarkable albeit unlucky women—Laverne DeFazio and Shirley Feeney. Remember milk and Pepsi? Moon pies? Lenny and Squiggy's entrances? Laverne's trademark *L*? How about the opening dance sequence?

The following dance and the accompanying advanced *Laverne and Shirley* moves should be done only with the best of friends—and try to keep a sense of homage and respect. As the sutra says, when you recline like the Buddha, you become like the Buddha.

And when you dance like Laverne and Shirley, you become like Laverne and Shirley.

Preparation: This dance may be performed anywhere, but for heightened effect, use the recommended settings (e.g. on a tour of a brewery in Milwaukee, outside a stoop on the streets of New York, etc.). Stretching is recommended, but not required.

For added pleasure, wear the following letter on your chest over your left side: *L*

1. Find a partner.
2. Decide who will be Laverne and who will be Shirley. This is important in order to synchronize moves. If there is argument over this decision, play Scissors, Paper, Rock to make the choice.
3. Begin the dance from a stationary position. Stand together, outside the front stoop of your apartment building.
4. Join arms.
5. Begin the count, "One, two, three, four, five, six, seven, eight," and with each number, leading first with the right leg and then with the left, take eight corresponding steps.
6. At "Schlemeil," stop. Shirley should, again leading with the right, take one step forward.
7. When "Schlemazel" is spoken, Shirley should step back, while Laverne steps forward,

Warning Note: *Before attempting the eighth-step, Laverne should withdraw her foot and be in a standing position. Any imbalance for steps eight and nine can be disastrous. Steps eight and nine occur simultaneously with the words "Hassenpfeffer" and "incorporated," respectively.*

8. Shirley bends at the knees.
9. Laverne bends at the knees.
10. Sing, "We're gonna do it!"

Advanced *LAVERNE AND SHIRLEY* Moves

1. With your partner, arrange the exact time for his or her return to the apartment. Synchronize watches. A few moments before your partner returns through the front door, get in the closet. At the appointed moment, open the closet door. Your partner should have opened the front door at exactly the same moment, and the two doors, as well as the two of you, should have collided. Look at each other with bewilderment as to why one of you was standing in a closet with the door shut, and then smile.

Note: The closet door and the front door must be right next to each other, otherwise the effect is lost.

2. Pull a bat on your landlady.
3. Ride a forklift.
4. Blow up a rubber glove, place it atop a bottle of beer moving down a conveyor belt, and wave bye-bye. Alternately, look off in the distance and run a single finger across your chin.

"And now a Muppet newsflash."
Muppet newscaster, *The Muppet Show*

"Like sands through the hourglass, so are the days of our lives."
Voice Over, *Days of Our Lives*

"Guess who! . . . Hahahahaha Hahahahaha haguguguguguguh!"
Woody Woodpecker, *The Woody Woodpecker Show*

"Spanning the globe to bring you the constant variety of sport—the thrill of victory, and the agony of defeat. The human drama of athletic competition! This is *ABC's Wide World of Sports!*"
Jim McKay, *ABC's Wide World of Sports*

"Ten years ago, in 1972, a crack commando unit was sent to prison by a military court for a crime they didn't commit. These men promptly escaped a maximum security stockade to the Los Angeles underground. Today, still wanted by the government, they survive as soldiers of fortune. If you have a problem, if no one else can help, and if you can find them, maybe you can hire *The A-Team.*"
Voice Over, *The A-Team*

37 Things That Bart Simpson Has Written on the Chalkboard at the Beginning of THE SIMPSONS

In 1990, the anti-Bradys were born in the form of *The Simpsons*. Bart, of course, was the rebel, the proud underachiever whom all could identify with. Here are 37 lessons he learned the hard way, as seen during the hilarious opening credits.

Why 37? Because we only liked 37 of them.

1. They are laughing at me, not with me.
2. I will not fake my way through life.
3. I will not do that thing with my tongue.
4. I will not call my teacher Hot Cakes.
5. I will not yell "fire" in a crowded classroom.
6. I will not encourage others to fly.
7. Tar is not a plaything.
8. I will not Xerox my butt.
9. I will not instigate revolution.
10. I will not draw naked ladies in class.
11. I did not see Elvis.
12. I will not trade pants with others.
13. I will not drive the principal's car.
14. I will not pledge allegiance to Bart.
15. I will not sell school property.
16. Spitwads are not free speech.
17. A burp is not an answer.
18. I will not get very far with this attitude.
19. I will not belch the National Anthem.
20. I will not sell land in Florida.
21. I will not grease the monkey bars.
22. I will not hide behind the Fifth Amendment.
23. Hamsters cannot fly.
24. I am not a dentist.
25. Underwear should be worn on the inside.
26. I will not torment the emotionally frail.
27. I will not expose the ignorance of the faculty.
28. I will not conduct my own fire drills.
29. This punishment is not boring and meaningless.
30. I will not prescribe medication.
31. I will not bury the new kid.
32. I will not bring sheep to class.
33. I will not eat things for money.
34. I will not yell "She's dead" during roll call.
35. The principal's toupee is not a frisbee.
36. Goldfish don't bounce.
37. I will finish what I star

"This is my boss, Jonathan Hart, a self-made millionaire. He's quite a guy. This is Mrs. H—she's gorgeous. What a tcriffic lady. By the way, my name's Max. I take care of both of 'em. 'Cause when they met, it was murder."
Max, *Hart to Hart*

"Knight Rider, a shadowy flight into the dangerous world of a man who does not exist. Michael Knight, a young loner on a crusade to champion the cause of the innocent, the helpless, the powerless in a world of criminals who operate above the law."
Voice Over, *Knight Rider*

"Try this for a deep dark secret: The great detective Remington Steele—he doesn't exist. I invented him. Follow: I'd always loved excitement, so I studied and apprenticed, and put my name on an office. But absolutely no one knocked on my door. A female private investigator seemed so . . . feminine. So I invented a superior. A decidedly masculine superior. Suddenly there were cases around the block. It was working like a charm. Until the day *he* walked in, with his blue eyes and mysterious past. And before I knew it, he assumed Remington Steele's identity. Now I do the work, and he takes the bows. It's a dangerous way to live, but as long as people buy it, I can get the job done. We never mix business with pleasure. Well, almost never. I don't even know his real name."
Laura Holt, *Remington Steele*

"It's so good to see all your bright faces out in front of the TV set. We're going to have a great time today—oh noooooooooooooooooo!"
Mr. Bill, *"The Mr. Bill Show," Saturday Night Live*

"Hey hey hey! Its Faaaaaaaaaat Albert!"
Fat Albert, *Fat Albert*

"You got big dreams? You want fame? Well, fame costs. And right here is where you start paying. In sweat."
Debbie Allen, *Fame*

14

"It's a beautiful day in the neighborhood
A beautiful day for a neighbor
Would you be mine? Could you be mine?
I married a woman said she was rich
  Spent all her money, walked out on the bitch
  Would you be mine? Could you be mine?
  Won't you be my neighbor?"

Mr.   Robinson, *"Mr.   Robinson's Neighborhood," Saturday Night Live*

"Dee plane! Dee plane!"
Tattoo, *Fantasy Island*

THE OFFICIAL SONGBOOK SECTION

n this chapter you will find the finest in TV theme songs and lyrics. Here are the actual words to songs we came to know by heart, as well as songs we never even heard the words to as TV viewers (usually because they were so bad that they weren't ever sung).

You know the tunes, just sing along. Or memorize the words and impress your friends!

● ● ● ● ● ● ● ● ● ● ● ● ● ● ● ● ●

THREE'S COMPANY Theme

Based on a British comedy, *A Man About the House, Three's Company* starred John Ritter as Jack Tripper, Joyce DeWitt as Janet Wood, Suzanne Somers as Chrissy Snow, and Norman Fell as Mr. Roper and later, Don Knotts as Mr. Furley. It was one of the worst sitcoms of all time and it ran, unbelievably, from 1977–1984.

> *Come and knock on our door*
> *(Come and knock on our door)*
> *We've been waiting for you*
> *(We've been waiting for you)*
> *Where the kisses are hers and hers and his,*
> *Three's company, too!*

Three's company, too!

Come and dance on our floor
(Come and dance on our floor)
Take a step that is new
(Take a step that is new)
We've a lovable place that needs your face,
Three's company, too!

Bridge: You'll see that life is a frolic and laughter is calling for
   you.
Down at our rendezvous
Three's company, too!

THE LOVE BOAT Theme

The Love Boat brought us years of love, passion, and guest stars who we'd eventually see on *Fantasy Island.*

Here are the classic words to the *Love Boat* theme, to bring you back that feeling of setting sail again.

Love
Exciting and new
Come aboard
We're expecting you
And love
Life's sweetest reward
Let it float
It floats back to you
The Love Boat
Soon will be making another run
The Love Boat
Promises something for everyone
Set a course for adventure,
   your mind on a new romance
And love
Won't hurt anymore
It's a friendly smile
On an open shore
It's loooooooooove
Welcome aboard it's looooo-ooooo-ooove!

The Previously Unknown Words to the *I DREAM OF JEANNIE* Theme

From 1965-1970 (NBC), Major Tony Nelson (a thinner, gentler Larry Hagman) thought he was in control, but we knew who wore the baggy pants and fez on *I Dream of Jeannie*—Jeannie herself (Barbara Eden) With that in mind, these lyrics—lyrics that were never sung—take on new meaning.

Jeannie, fresh as a daisy!
Just love how she obeys me,
Does things that just amaze me so.
She smiles—presto! The rain goes.
She blinks—up come the rainbows.
Cars stop, even the train goes slow
When she goes by!
She paints sunshine on every rafter,
Sprinkles the air with laughter,
We're close as a quarter after three.
There's no one like Jeannie
I'll introduce 'er to you
But it's no use, sir
'Cause my Jeannie's in love with me!

The Previously Unknown Words to the *STAR TREK THEME*

We're thankful that these words were never sung. If they had been, thousands—no, millions—of Trekkies might have been so disgusted that they never would have tuned in. Written by Gene Roddenberry in 1966, they explain a lot about his real intentions for *Star Trek* (1966–1969, NBC). It was to be a soap opera in space.

Beyond the rim of starlight
My love is wandering in star   flight
I know he'll find in star-clustered reaches love
Strange love, a star woman teaches
I know his journey ends never
His star trek will go on forever
But tell him while he wanders his starry sea
Remember, remember me!

The Unknown Words to THE ODD COUPLE Theme

The Odd Couple (1970–1975, ABC) was based on Neil Simon's play of the same name. You remember the tune but not the lyrics, right? That's because they were never sung.

No matter where they go
They are known as the couple
They're never seen alone
So they're known as the couple
As I've indicated
They are never quite separated
They are peas in a pod.
Don't you think that it's odd?
Their habits I confess,
None can guess with the couple.
If one says no, it's yes,
More or less, with the couple
But they're laugh provoking
Yet they really don't know they're
*   joking*
Don't you find
When love is blind
It's kind of odd!

The Largely Unknown Words to the BEWITCHED Theme

Bewitched, betwitched, you've got me in your spell
Bewitched, bewitched, you know your craft so well.
Before I knew what you were doing
I looked into your eyes
That brand of woo you've been brewing
Took me by surprise
You witch, you witch, one thing is for sure
That stuff you pitch, just hasn't got a
*   cure*
My heart was under lock and key
But somehow it got unhitched
I never thought my heart could be had
But now I'm caught and I'm kinda glad
To be bewitched!

NANU NANU: GREETINGS, ENTRANCES, AND EXCLAMATIONS

*F*irst impressions are important. We learned this from our teachers, our parents, and our bosses—but mostly from Bugs Bunny and Lenny and Squiggy. If you want to get everyone's attention, if you want to go anywhere in life, you've got to have your greetings down.

Here, from TV professionals, are the memorable greetings, entrances, and exclamations that made such a significant impression on all of us, along with information on how to greet people boarding a cruise ship, *Schoolhouse Rock's* "Interjections," and much more.

With the knowledge residing in this chapter, you'll never enter a room unnoticed again.

● ● ● ● ● ● ● ● ● ● ● ● ● ● ● ● ●

Hub-bi frub-biends!
   Zoom

"Youuuuu rannng?"
   Lurch, *The Addams Family*

"Bedeebeedeebeedeebeedeebee what's up, Buck?"
   Twiki, *Buck Rogers in the 25th Century*

"It's Charlie, Angels. Time to go to work."
   Charlie, *Charlie's Angels*

"Eh, what's up, doc?"
Bugs Bunny, *The Bugs Bunny/Road Runner Show*

"It's a beautiful day in the neighborhood,
A beautiful day for a neighbor
Would you be mine?
Could you be mine?
Won't you be my neighbor?"
Mr. Rogers, *Mr. Rogers' Neighborhood*

"Grandma, these are the Cunninghams—a very kind of Midwestern family. Cunninghams, this is my grandma—Mrs. Nussbaum."
Fonzie, *Happy Days*

"Oh, hi! Elmo is looking for someone to tickle."
Elmo, *Sesame Street*

"Oh Prickle! We're in a pickle!"
Gumby, *Gumby*

"No way, Mr. Man Driver!"
Marcia Brady, *The Brady Bunch*

"Oh no! I been CHiPed!"
Speeding Driver, *CHiPS*

"Marcia, Marcia, Marcia!"
Jan Brady, *The Brady Bunch*

"Oh, come on, Thelma Lou. Put two and two together. Read the handwritin' on the wall. Blow away the smoke and look at the fire!"
Barney Fife, *The Andy Griffith Show*

SHIRLEY: I'm telling you, Laverne, this whole thing is sick and morbid.
LENNY AND SQUIGGY (*entering*): Hello!
Laverne and Shirley

"It's the plumber. I've come to fix the sink."
The Plumber, *Electric Company*

"Show time, gentle people!"
Lydia, *Fame*

Colonel Potterisms

Colonel Sherman Potter had a way with words. A career officer who had served proudly in WWII (the second war to end all wars), Potter came to the 4077th *M*A*S*H* after the death of Colonel Blake (MacLean Stevenson).

One of Colonel Potter's best coping mechanisms was his creative vocabulary. Some of the best examples follow.

Horse hockey!
Mule fritters!
Monkey muffins!
Buffalo bagels!
Buffalo chips!
Pigeon pellets!
Pony pucks!
Beaver biscuits!
Cow cookies!
Bull cookies!
Road apples!
Sufferin' saddlesoap!
Sufferin' sheepdip!
Shiverin' shinbones!
Sweet limburger!
Sweet Nefertiti!
Geeze Louise!
Great Caesar's ghost!
Great Mother McCree!
Where in the name of Carrie's corset . . .
What in the name of Sweet Fanny Adams . . .
What in the name of Marco "Blessed" Polo . . .
What in the name of Samuel Hill . . .
What in the name of Great Caesar's salad . . .
What in the name of George Armstrong Custer . . .

SCHOOLHOUSE ROCK's Interjections!

Schoolhouse Rock was created to fill the time between cartoons on Saturday mornings with something other than advertising over-sweetened breakfast cereals and games by Milton Bradley—they wanted to use the time to teach history, government, math, science, and grammar. Thus, *Schoolhouse Rock* was born. It did the job. Because of *Schoolhouse Rock* a generation of youth now knows the preamble to the Constitution by heart, how a bill becomes a law (page 82), where to find conjunctions (page 81), and what an interjection is. For those who don't remember, here's a refresher course.

"Cough! Cough! Cough!"

When Reginald was home with flu (uh huh)
The doctor knew just what to do:
He cured the infection,
With one small injection,
While Reginald uttered some interjections:

"Hey! That smarts!
Ouch! That hurts!
Yow! That's not fair, giving a guy a shot down there!"

Interjections—"Hey!"
Show excitement—"Yow!"
Or emotion—"Ouch!"
They're generally set apart from a sentence
By an exclamation point,
Or by a comma when the feeling's not as strong. Mmmm . . .

Though Geraldine played hard to get (uh huh)
Geraldo knew he'd woo her yet.
He showed his affection,
Despite her objections,
And Geraldine hollered some interjections:

"Well! You've got some nerve!
Oh! I've never been so insulted in all my life!
Hey! You're kinda cute!"

Interjections—"Well!"
Show excitement—"Oh!"
Or emotion—"Hey!"
They're generally set apart from a sentence
By an exclamation point,
Or by a comma when the feeling's not as strong.

So when you're happy—"Hurray!"
Or sad—"Aw!"
Or frightened—"Eeeeeek!"
Or mad—"Rats!"
Or excited—"Wow!"
Or glad—"Hey!"

An interjection starts a sentence right!
The game was tied at seven all (uh huh)
When Franklin found he had the ball.
He made a connection,
In the other direction,
And the crowd starting shouting out interjections:

"Aw! You threw the wrong way!
Darn! You just lost the game!
Hurray! I'm for the other team!"

Interjections—"Aw!"
Show excitement,—"Darn!"
Or emotion.—"Hurray!"
They're generally set apart from a sentence
By an exclamation point,
Or by a comma when the feeling's not as strong.

So when you're happy—"Hurray!"
Or sad—"Aw!"
Or frightened—"Eeeeeek!"
Or mad—"Rats!"
Or excited—"Wow!"
Or glad—"Hey!"
An interjection starts a sentence right!

Interjections—"Hey!"
Show excitement,—"Hey!"
Or emotion.—"Hey!"
They're generally set apart from a sentence
By an exclamation point
Or by a comma when the feeling's not as strong.

Interjections!
Show excitement!
Or emotion!
Hallelujah!
Hallelujah!
Hallelujah . . . yea!!

"Darn, that's the end."

Holy Robin Exclamations!

Ah, Batman. From 1966 to 1968 Batman and Robin brought us weekly cliff-hangers, fabulous costumes, and a lot of camp. We remember Burt Ward (Robin) for his TV legacy: holyisms.

HOLY RAVIOLI!

HOLY HORS D' OEUVRES!

HOLY HAREM!

HOLY SAFARI!

HOLY CAFFEINE!

HOLY STUFFING!

HOLY HEADACHE!

HOLY DIAMOND DOSING GAS!

HOLY TROLLS AND GOBLINS!

HOLY SERPENTINE!

HOLY HEADLINES!

HOLY RED HERRING!

HOLY HYPNOTISM!

HOLY JACK-IN-THE-BOX!

HOLY FATE WORSE THAN DEATH!

HOLY COLD FACTS!

HOLY SHOT GUN WEDDINGS!

How to Greet People Boarding a Cruise Ship

Let's pretend Julie McCoy is off on a couple of weeks' sick leave. You are her cousin and are filling in for her while she recovers from _(noun)_ _(fixation)_ her at the Betty _(last name of a President)_ Clinic.

Practice greeting passengers as they arrive on the Love Boat. Be courteous. Be honorable. And above all, be perky!

You: Hi, I'm _(proper name)_ McCoy, your cruise director. Welcome to our _(theme)_ cruise.

Passenger: Yes, hello, nice to meet you. What a _(adjective)_ ship you have.

You: Why, thank you. I was just about to say the same about you.

Passenger: My name is _(proper name)_ Johnson. And this is my—

You: Let me guess . . . your _(type of pet or relative)_.

Passenger: No. Actually _(pronoun)_'s my _(type of pet or relative)_ Robyn _(last name)_. But perhaps one day I can convince _(pronoun)_ to _(active verb)_ and be my _(different type of pet or relative)_.

You: Well, you and your _(type of pet or relative)_ will have a _(adjective)_ time aboard. The Love Boat always seems to have that effect on people. It's like _(abstract noun)_ and _(abstract noun)_.

Passenger: Could you tell me, when do we arrive at Puerto _(foreign name)_?

You: Well, it looks like we're scheduled to arrive at Puerto _(foreign name)_ on _(holiday)_. And then at Puerto _(foreign name)_ on _(holiday)_. So we should be at Puerto _(foreign name)_ by _(day)_.

Passenger: Oh. We're very _(adjective—state of mind)_ about gettting there.

You: Well, in the meantime, may I suggest some _(adjective)_ and _(adjective)_ activities for you and your _(type of pet or relative)_ to enjoy along the way?

Passenger: Perhaps later. For now we just want to go to our cabin. Could you tell us where the _(exotic dance)_ deck is?

You: _(exclamation)_! You just _(verb)_ down past the _(tropical drink)_ deck and then _(number)_ floors down, after the _(possesive noun)_ cabana and past the Doctor's _(type of room)_, then take a left and you'll see a picture of Captain _(name of dictator)_. Turn right, and yours is number twelve.

Passenger: Thank you!

You: Oh, no, _(exclamation)_ you!

The "Welcome to Puerta Vallarta" Speech by Julie McCoy, Your Love Boat Cruise Director

Certain speeches stand above all others in our collective memory—Martin Luther King's "I Have a Dream" speech; Lincoln's "Gettysburg Address"; and now, Julie McCoy's "Welcome to Puerta Vallarta" announcement. Every Saturday night, from 1977 to 1984, Julie McCoy gave some variation of this speech (unless it was a special cruise to, say, Alaska or Vancouver). The speech always came after the midpoint of the show (the point at which all the happy couples were fighting it out), and it typifies everything that was important in the late 70s and early 80s—beauty, food, and shopping.

Enjoy your stay, and don't forget to try the parasailing.

"Buenos dias, señoras y señoritas. We will be docking shortly in Puerta Vallarta, Mexico's haven for pleasure seekers. During your stay, enjoy the glorious sun-drenched beaches, delightful cantinas, or shopping in the many colorful boutiques. Whatever your pleasure, the good life awaits you."

"Konichiwa, Angin-San."
Pora naga-sun, *Shogun*

"Bristle Hound's the name, savin' sheep's my game."
Bristle Hound,
The Laff-a-Lympics

"Hello! Touché Turtle here. Hero extra-ordinary and all that sort of stuff."
Touché Turtle,
The Laff-a-Lympics

"Morning, everybody! Sorry I'm late—unless I'm not."
Herb Tarlick,
WKRP in Cincinnati

"Good morning, Angels. You're all looking chipper!"

Woodville, *Charlie's Angels*

"Mork calling Orson. Come in, Orson. Come in, Orson. Yoo-hoo! Come in, Hippo Hips!"

Mork, *Mork and Mindy*

"Nanu nanu."

Mork, *Mork and Mindy*

SMILES, EVERYONE, SMILES:
CATCH PHRASES AND
OTHER WORDS TO REMEMBER

*C*ritics of the electronic age in general, and television in particular, tell us that it must be dangerous to embrace the language of TV as whole-heartedly as we have. They worry that it will blur the lines of reality. Don't we begin to think that *Fantasy Island* might in fact be a nice place to visit, that the Brady Bunch wouldn't be such annoying neighbors after all, and that if all cops had been as thorough as Columbo, the O.J. trial would have gone differently?

The answer is no. We know the difference between TV and reality, the difference between words uttered by our friends and family and those uttered by fictional characters. We know that *Gilligan's Island* was really a California studio, that the people on *The Love Boat* were actually actors from other bad shows, and that Mork couldn't really have come from a planet called Ork (Ork is way too far away).

Here are the words we've made our own over the years—catch phrases, sayings, and lines to remember. These are the lines that have stayed with us, words that have come to define our finest moments.

● ● ● ● ● ● ● ● ● ● ● ● ● ● ● ● ● ●

"Oh my nose! Oh my nose!"
Marcia Brady, *The Brady Bunch*

"Zoinks! The ghost! Scoooooooooob! Let's get outtaheeeeeeeere!"
Shaggy, *Scooby Doo*

"Jinkies!"
> **Velma,** *Scooby Doo*

"Rooby rooby roooo!"
> **Scooby,** *Scooby Doo*

"It's so crazy, it just might work!"
> **Fred,** *Scooby Doo*

"Boy! I say . . . I say boy!"
> **Foghorn Leghorn,** *The Bugs Bunny/Road Runner Show*

"Shazbat!"
> **Mork,** *Mork and Mindy*

"Outtasight!"
> **Isaac,** *The Love Boat*

"DY-NO-MITE!"
> **Jimmy,** *Good Times*

"Wunnerful, wunnerful."
> **Lawrence Welk,** *The Lawrence Welk Show*

"Shazam!"
> **Gomer Pyle,** *Gomer Pyle, U.S.M.C.*

"Sit on it."
> **The Cast,** *Happy Days*

"Correctamundo!"
> **Fonzie,** *Happy Days*

"It's purrrrrrrrfect."
> **Catwoman,** *Batman*

"Oh, Lucy! You're not getting another idea, are you?"
> **Ethel Mertz,** *I Love Lucy*

"Heavens to Mergatroid!"
Snagglepuss, *The Laff-a-Lympics*

"Kiss my grits!"
Flo Castleberry, *Alice*

"Go 'head—'splain!"
Ricky Ricardo, *I Love Lucy*

"Nip it! Nip it in the bud!"
Barney Fife, *The Andy Griffith Show*

"Up your nose wit' a rubber hose!"
Arnold Horshack, *Welcome Back, Kotter*

"Fox-es!"
The Festrunk Brothers, *Saturday Night Live*

"What'chu talkin' 'bout, Willis?"
Arnold Drummond, *Diff'rent Strokes*

"Speedy dellvery to you!"
Mr. McFeeley, *Mr. Rogers' Neighborhood*

"Yabba-dabba-doo!"
Fred Flintstone, *The Flintstones*

"Heeey, Boo Boo!"
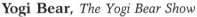
Yogi Bear, *The Yogi Bear Show*

"Aw, chee whiz!"
Archie Bunker, *All in the Family*

"Me want cookie!"
Cookie Monster, *Sesame Street*

Commercial Break —

"I go cuckoo for Cocoa Puffs!"
Cocoa Puffs commercial

"They're grrrrrrrrreeaaatt!"
Frosted Flakes commercial

"They're magically delicious!"
Lucky Charms commercial

"Silly Rabbit! Trix are for kids!"
Trix commercial

"I'm hot!
I'm thirsty!
Hey! Kool Aid!"
Kool Aid commercial

Twoallbeefpattiesspecialsaucelettucecheesepick-
lesonionsonasesameseedbun!
McDonald's commercial

The night-time sniffling, sneezing, coughing, aching,
stuffy head, fever, so-you-can-rest medicine.
Nyquil commercial

Strong enough for a man, but made for a woman.
Secret commercial

In-da-ges-tion.
Pepto Bismol commercial

But wait!
Ginsu Knives commercial

I'm not a doctor, but I play one on TV.
Excedrin commercial

I've fallen and I can't get up!
Life Call commercial

Indianaisms, from David Letterman

David Letterman is from Indiana, as he likes to remind us. He brings up this fact at least once a week, usually as a complete non sequitur—"Ask, or as we say in Indiana . . . ax." For those who love Dave in his old incarnation, *Late Night with David Letterman* (1982–1993), the following is a guide to "talking Hoosier."

Bush—or as we say in Indiana—Boosh!
Extra—or as we say in Indiana—extree!
Illinois—or as we say in Indiana—Illinoiz!
Italian—or as we say in Indiana—Eye-talian!
Mosquitos—or as we say in Indiana—skeeters!
Nuclear—or as we say in Indiana—nuc-u-lar!
President Clinton—or as we say in Indiana—Pars'dent Clinton!
Pumpkin—or as we say in Indiana—punkin!
Show business—or as we say in Indiana—show bidness!
Similar—or as we say in Indiana—sim-u-lar!
Special—or as we say in Indiana—spay-shul!
Statistics—or as we say in Indiana—suh-tistics!
Veteran—or as we say in Indiana—vet'rin!
Washington—or as we say in Indiana—Warshington!

32

I'm also a client!
Hair Club for Men commercial

Calgon! Take me away!
Calgon commercial

"Nothing comes between me and my Calvins."
Brooke Shields,

Calvin Klein commercial

The Double-Take

When you spot something that makes you want to do a double- take (a beautiful man or woman; a person you thought was gone, but who quickly returned), here's the routine.

1. Turn away slowly. Then, realizing what you've seen, move your head back and forth from one side to the other, and say, "Eeeyaah! Eeeyaah! Eeeyaah! Aoooooooooooogah!"

2. If it is a beautiful person you see, raise your hands like a begging dog, and say, "Yip! Yip! Yip!" then pant, and howl, "Ahooooooooooo!"

Four out of five dentists surveyed recommend Trident sugarless gum for their patients who chew gum!
Trident commercial

Meegle? Oh, Gleem! You held it upside down!
Gleem commercial

I'm not gonna try it. You try it!
I'm not gonna try it.
Let's get Mikey!
He won't eat it, he hates everything."
He likes it! Hey, Mikey!
Life commercial

You sank my battleship!
Battleship commercial

Pret-ty snea-ky, sis.
Connect Four commercial

Operation—the wacky doctor's game! . . . Don't touch the sides!
Operation commercial

"Where's the beef?"
Clara Peller, Burger King commercial

— And Now, Back to Our Chapter

"Book 'em, DanO!"
Steve McGarrett, *Hawaii Five-0*

"Well excuuuuuuuuuuuuuuuuuse me!"
Steve Martin, *Saturday Night Live*

"One Adam-12, one Adam-12, see the man."
Dispatcher, *Adam-12*

"Who loves ya, baby?"
Kojak, *Kojak*

"It's the old bullet-proof cummerbund-in-the-tuxedo trick!"
Maxwell Smart, *Get Smart*

"Hornet gun, check. Hornet sting, check. Let's roll, Kato!"
Green Hornet, *Green Hornet*

"Michael, my sensors detect a structure just over the next rise."
Kitt, *Knight Rider*

"I tawt I taw a puddy tat! . . . I did! I did! I did see a puddy tat!"
Tweety Bird, *The Bugs Bunny/Road Runner Show*

"Jane! Stop this crazy thing! Jane! Jaaaaaaaannne!"
George Jetson, *The Jetsons*

"I yam what I yam."
Popeye, *Popeye the Sailor Man*

"I beg your pardon, sir, but there is one more thing . . ."
Columbo, *Columbo*

"Holy vanishing point! They've all disappeared!"
Robin, *The Superfriends*

How to Make Classic TV Noises

Television has given us many wonderful things over the years—laughter, music, wisdom, friends to come home to—and a wonderful variety of sounds to cherish. Here's a guide to making some of them in your own home.

STAR TREK Noises

THE TURBO LIFT

1. When walking through a doorway, say "Shhhhht!" quickly, just before you step into the doorway to open the door.

2. Step into the doorway.

3. When you walk through the other side of the doorway, say "Shhhhht!" again to close the door.

BATTLE

1. Have a friend say "Wooooop! (*pause*) Wooooop!" repeatedly.

2. Pretend to press the intercom. Whistle "ooo—wweee—ooop!" This is the intercom sound.

3. Say, "This is the Captain speaking. All hands to battle stations. This is a red alert. This is not a drill. Repeat, this is not a drill."

4. Say, "Fire photon torpedos." Make six rapid-fire "cue! cue! cue! cue! cue! cue!" sounds.

5. Make a sound like a ship blowing up.

Cartoon Noises

THE LATHER NOISE

1. Relax your cheeks, and pinch both of them—your right with your right thumb and forefinger and your left with your left thumb and forefinger.

2. Holding your cheeks, and keeping your face relaxed, waggle your cheeks in and out.

3. Congratulations! You've made the lather noise. Make this sound when pretending to wash someone's hair, shaving, or taking a bath.

"Great Scott!"
        Superman, *The Superfriends*

"Great Hera!"
        Wonder Woman, *The Superfriends*

How to React When the Warp Core Is Under Stress and the Klingons are Attacking, According to Scotty

Before Bob Vila, before Tim Allen, there was Commander Montgomery Scott. Scotty was the original handyman—a hard-working, hard-drinking engineer who could fix anything in about 1/16 the time it would take a normal human to fix it. As the *Enterprise's* chief engineer between the years of its original mission (1966–1969), Scotty rarely left the bridge or the engine room—but when he did, he did it with style. Moreover, Scotty was one of the few red-shirted officers to survive—most other red shirts could be counted on to die, and fast.

Here's Scotty at his best—his personal list of what to do when the warp core is "gonna blow!"

1. As soon as you realize that the warp core is going to blow, tell the Captain. He'll ask you how much time it will take to fix things. Tell him you'll need a lot more time than you actually do. The Captain will then tell you, "That's not good enough, Scotty. You'll have to do better." He'll give you a matter of minutes.

2. Climb into the Jeffries tube with a tool or two. It doesn't matter which tools—nobody but you understands what you're doing, anyway.

3. While you're "working on it," pretend to shimmy and shake every so often, as if your ship has been hit with a phaser or photon torpedo. They'll be doing the same thing on the bridge. Think, "Why didn't I ever install those seatbelts?"

4. When the engine is again online and the ship is warping away at top speed, inform the Captain that "She canna take much more o' this! She's breakin' apart!" The Captain likes to hear this, and he'll ask you to "hold her together just a little bit longer." Tell the Captain you'll do what you can. Smoke a cigarette and relax.

5. When the ship is out of danger, tell the Captain you'll need "at least twelve hours to complete repairs." Finish the job in three hours.

6. Leave the engine room and let the junior engineers fix the warp core. Go back to your quarters, replicate a pint of Romulan ale, and congratulate yourself on another job well done!

"Arriba, arriba! Andale! Arriba, arriba! Yeehaw!"
Speedy Gonzales, *The Bugs Bunny/Road Runner Show*

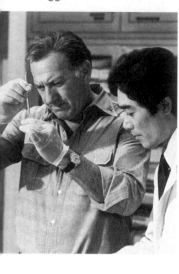

"Something here doesn't add up."
Quincy, *Quincy*

"Oooh! Oooh! Oohoohoohooh!"
Horshack, *Welcome Back, Kotter*

"Les bow-wow-wow. Les bow. Les wow."
Pepe le Pew, *The Bugs Bunny/Road Runner Show*

"Be vewy vewy quiet. Weew hunting wabbits."
Elmer Fudd, *The Bugs Bunny/Road Runner Show*

"Oooooh! He don't know me vewy well, do he?"
Tweety Bird, *The Bugs Bunny/Road Runner Show*

"Exciting, isn't it?"
Droopy, *Droopy*

"Smile! You're on *Candid Camera!*"
Allan Funt, *Candid Camera*

"Smiles, everyone! Smiles!"
Mr. Roarke, *Fantasy Island*

"Let's play the Feud!"
Richard Dawson, *Family Feud*

"Joker—joker—joker!"
Jack Barry, *The Joker's Wild*

"And the actual price of your showcase is . . ."
Bob Barker, *The Price Is Right*

"Y'all better not go to the refrigerator now."
The Balladeer, *The Dukes of Hazzard*

"Survey says . . ."
Richard Dawson, *Family Feud*

"What? What is it, girl?"
Jimmy, *Lassie*

"I love a hap-py crew!"
Gopher, *The Love Boat*

"And hey! Let's be careful out there."
Sergeant Esterhaus, *Hill Street Blues*

DO ALL YOUR HOMEWORK, AND TELL EVERYONE YOU COME FROM FRANCE: TIMELESS WISDOM AND UNCOMMON SENSE

Years ago there were Confucius, Buddha, Christ, and Plato, all of whom preached the wisdom of living. Sometimes this wisdom was timeless—"Thou shalt not commit murder." And sometimes it wasn't—"Confucius say man who live in grass hut and tend oxen live in grass hut and tend oxen."

In any event, these are the things we have learned—words of wisdom and uncommon sense that have been given to us, overtly and covertly—during our many thousands of hours of watching TV.

These lessons have come to us in many forms, over many years. They came to us as children when we watched *Mr. Rogers' Neighborhood* and *Zoom*. They came to us as teenagers when we soaked in *The A-Team, Laverne and Shirley,* and *M*A*S*H*. And they still come to us as adults. They will continue to come, like the Energizer Bunny, whenever we watch TV.

These are the things we have learned from sages, aliens, dimwits, bartenders, waitresses, detectives, taxi drivers, news anchormen, cruise directors, Bradys, Huxtables, Ewings, Vulcans, and Muppets.

Welcome to TV 101.

● ● ● ● ● ● ● ● ● ● ● ● ● ● ● ● ●

"It's not easy being green."
Kermit the Frog, *Sesame Street*

"There's a time to be Daniel Boone, and there's a time to be a plumber."
MacGyver, *MacGyver*

"Live long and prosper."
Mr. Spock, *Star Trek*

Weebles wobble but they don't fall down.
Weebles commercial

"A watched cauldron never boils."
Morticia Addams, *The Addams Family*

"Most opportunities are lost, because they are not recognized."
Mr. Roarke, *Fantasy Island*

Fish out of water frequently end up in the frying pan.
Fantasy Island

"Fate has a nasty way of popping up and wagging its long, bony finger under your nose. Sometimes it's a squeaker at seventy miles an hour. Sometimes it's a plane you miss that never makes it back from the Bermuda Triangle. But whatever it is, you always get the message: It's time to stop taking your good luck for granted."
Thomas Magnum, *Magnum P.I.*

"One man can make a difference, Michael."
Devon, *Knight Rider*

"Sneaky ways are always the best ways."
Julie McCoy, *The Love Boat*

"Money's not made layin' in the shade."
Ricardo, *Miami Vice*

"It's unwise to condemn what we don't understand."
Batman and Robin, *Batman*

"We've all got a little Obi Wan Kenobi in us."
Jim Kowalski, *Taxi*

How to Use Common Household Items to Save Your Neck, Like MACGYVER

MacGyver (Richard Dean Anderson) was the ultimate action hero. His first instinct, whenever he was in a dangerous situation—trapped by terrorists, tied to a bomb—was to stop, look, listen, and think. And usually, with a little imagination, whatever happened to be lying around, and a basic knowledge of science and common sense, he could forge his way to safety. Here are some of the more creative uses he taught us for common household items.

- [ ] Paper clips
  - Can be used for disarming missiles.
  - Can be used to hot-wire cars.
- [ ] Candy
  - Milk chocolate stops sulfuric acid leaks.
  - Gum wrappers (foil) make good fuses.
- [ ] Credit cards
  - Can be used to mess up traffic signals.
- [ ] Maps
  - Can be used to retrieve keys.
  - Can be used as peashooter-type weapons.
  - With duct tape, can be used to patch holes in hot air balloons.
- [ ] Belts
  - Can be used to make a car drive itself.
- [ ] Hoses
  - Can become flame throwers, with a metal pipe and a little gasoline.
  - Once melted, can be spread on a net and used as an ant repellant suit.
- [ ] Bombs
  - Cotton, starter fluid, and fertilizer make a nice one.
  - Hockey tickets can stop one from detonating.
- [ ] Empty guns
  - Can be used as wrenches.
- [ ] Spatula
  - If attached to a ceiling fan, sounds like a helicopter.
- [ ] Comb
  - Can be used with foil to sound like a siren.
- [ ] Umbrella
  - Can be used with a rope as a grappling hook.
- [ ] Mops
  - Loaded with pepper, can be used to stun a bad guy.

"It takes a big man to cry, but it takes a bigger man to laugh at that man."
Jack Handey, "Deep Thoughts," *Saturday Night Live*

"Individuality is fine . . . as long as we do it together."
Frank Burns, *M*A*S*H*

There's something about an Aqua Velva man.
Aqua Velva commercial

"You can tell a lot about things just by looking."
Jonesy, *The Waltons*

"Don't end up in a cement eggroll."
Chin Ho, *Hawaii Five-0*

"Sometimes when we lose, we win."
Carol Brady, *The Brady Bunch*

"You shouldn't put down a loser, Cindy . . . because you might be one yourself someday."
Carol Brady, *The Brady Bunch*

"You can't take a step forward with two feet on the ground."
Mike Brady, *The Brady Bunch*

Eight is enough to fill our lives with love.
Eight Is Enough

"When a man finds his way, heaven is gentle."
Caine, *Kung Fu*

"Become the calm and restful breeze that tames the violent sea."
Master Kan, *Kung Fu*

"The sun endures, the moon endures, life endures."
Master Po, *Kung Fu*

"The supple willow does not contend against the storm, yet it survives."
Master Kan, *Kung Fu*

"A Partridge never forgets."
Danny Partridge, *The Partridge Family*

"You know what I always say—'Somebody down there likes me.'"
Boris, *Rocky and Bullwinkle*

"He who quits and runs away will live to quit another day."
Corporal Agarn, *F-Troop*

"If a man don't grow, he dies."
Boss Hogg, *The Dukes of Hazzard*

"He who plays and runs away lives to play another day."
Bret Maverick, *Maverick*

"There's more than one way to please a lady."
Bret Maverick, *Maverick*

"Never play in a rigged game, unless you rig it yourself."
Bret Maverick, *Maverick*

"Don't take life too seriously. You'll never get out alive."
Bugs Bunny

SHIRLEY: There's more to life than taking bows.
DANNY: Not when you're an egomaniac with greasepaint in
    your blood.
The Partridge Family

"An insult to a man with no feelings is like hay fever to a man
with no nose."
Mork, *Mork and Mindy*

"A straight line may be the shortest distance between two
points, but it is by no means the most interesting."
The Doctor, *Doctor Who*

"Every fool knows you can't touch the stars, but it doesn't stop
them from trying."
Harry Stone, *Night Court*

"A horse is a horse, of course, of course."
Mr. Ed, *Mr. Ed*

"Due to the shape of the North American elk's esophagus, even if it could speak, it could not pronounce the word *lasagna*."
Cliff Clavin, *Cheers*

"It's what's under the hood that counts."
Brandon Walsh, *Beverly Hills 90210*

"If you've never worked an electric train, you haven't lived."
Super Dave, *Super Dave*

Words of Courage and Hope to Riding Hood Eaters, from FRACTURED FAIRY TALES

From 1959 to 1964, and in years of reruns thereafter, *Rocky and His Friends* and *The Bullwinkle Show* brought us a kind of wit and irony that an animated show never had before. They also brought us screwed-up versions of classic fairy tales, fables, and history, in the form of *Fractured Fairy Tales, Aesop and Son,* and *Peabody's Improbable History.*

One such fairy tale is "Riding Hoods Anonymous." In this retelling of "Little Red Riding Hood" the wolf has joined Riding Hoods Anonymous, and attempts to swear off eating Riding Hoods—but not grandmas. Throughout the episode he reads from a book entitled *Words of Courage and Hope to Riding Hood Eaters.* Here are some of those words.

I hereby swear that I'll be good.
I will not eat a Riding Hood.
When you see a Riding Hood,
Greet her as a friend you should.
When you are misunderstood,
Extend your hand to Riding Hood.
Stick with your promise not to eat—
Fight that urge for a Riding Hood treat!
Though Riding Hoods you may not munch,
There's nothing wrong with a grandma lunch!
When grandmas claim to be Riding Hoods,
Be a photographer in the woods.
Every day, in every way,
I am not eating Riding Hoods.

"Blackmail is a growth industry."
Sydney, *Melrose Place*

"I've been a kid, and I've been an adult. And believe me, adultery isn't what it's cracked up to be.
Danny Partridge, *The Partridge Family*

"You'll feel a lot better after a good bleeding."
Theodoric of York, *Saturday Night Live*

"When will I learn? The answers to life's problems aren't at the bottom of a bottle. They're on TV."
Homer Simpson, *The Simpsons*

"When a young girl drops out of sight, we worry."
Sergeant Joe Friday, *Dragnet*

"Anything is possible on Fantasy Island."
Mr. Roarke, *Fantasy Island*

NELSON: Don't do anything I wouldn't do.
MORK: Would you do this: Neegee, neegee . . . prrrrprrrr . . .
 chichchichchich . . . woof woof woof . . . negahbrrr . . . Ha ha!
NELSON: No.
MORK: Pity.
 Mork and Mindy

"Ladies and gentlemen, take my advice. Pull down your pants and slide on the ice."
Sidney Freedman, *M*A*S*H*

"Just do all of your homework and tell everyone you come from France."
Prymaat Conehead, *Saturday Night Live*

"TV is always right."
Homer Simpson, *The Simpsons*

There's no such thing as a routine expedition.
> ***Land of the Lost***

Never hunt ghosts without a snack.
> ***Scooby Doo***

Drive fast, talk to your car.
> ***Speed Buggy*** and ***Speed Racer***

Sea monsters are people, too.
> ***Sigmund the Sea Monster***

It's not size that matters, it's how you use it.
> ***Inch-High Private Eye***

Never buy things made by ACME.
> ***The Road Runner***

Corporations suck, even in the 23rd century.
> ***The Jetsons***

Cartoons need their exercise, too.
> ***The Laff-a-Lympics***

Everybody needs a good sidekick.
> ***Johnny Quest***

Never get accidentally launched into space.
> ***Josie and the Pussycats***

Only prehistoric hairballs and people named Charlie are allowed to have angels.
> ***Captain Caveman and the Teen Angels***

All I Ever Needed to Know I Learnerd from Sitcoms

Never give up.
I Love Lucy

Alternative lifestyles can be good.
The Addams Family

When in doubt, pretend to be gay, or dress in drag.
Bosom Buddies

Waitresses are people, too.
Alice

Life isn't easy, even with supernatural powers.
Bewitched

Liberal parents produce screwed-up kids, too.
Family Ties

It's important to have an office in the bathroom.
Happy Days

If you find a bottle on the beach, keep it.
I Dream of Jeannie

Good entrances are important.
Laverne and Shirley

Don't play ball in the house.
The Brady Bunch

Castaways get a lot of visitors.
Gilligan's Island

Sloppy roommates make good coroners.
The Odd Couple and **Quincy**

All I Ever Needed to Know I Learned from Adventure Shows

Everyone needs an angel.
Charlie's Angels

When in doubt, blow things up.
The A-Team

Don't oversleep.
Buck Rogers in the 25th Century

Brothers make good detectives.
The Hardy Boys and **Simon and Simon**

Cool theme music adds authority.
Dragnet

Control your anger.
The Incredible Hulk

Make do with what you've got.
MacGyver

Being a good cop isn't all pastel suits and cool sunglasses.
Miami Vice

Nothing is impossible.
Mission: Impossible

Whatever doesn't kill you will only make you stronger.
The Six Million Dollar Man

PARDON ME—DO YOU HAVE ANY GREY POUPON?: COSMIC QUESTIONS AND BAD POETRY

W hy are we here? Is there a higher power? If a tree falls in the forest and nobody's around to hear it, does it make a sound? What is the sound of one hand clapping? And of course, Mom, do you ever get that not-so-fresh feeling?

These are the cosmic questions we've had to wrestle with in our lives, questions without answers, but questions that we must each answer individually in order to move steadily through life.

This chapter brings to the forefront some of those difficult questions as posed by TV's wisest of the wise cops, cartoon characters, coaches, and others. And because they are equally thought-provoking, we've included some of TV's best poetic verses for your musings as well.

●●●●●●●●●●●●●●●●●

Questions

"Pardon me—do you have any Grey Poupon?"
Grey Poupon commercial

"Do you know what it's like to be chasing a guy on 43rd Street when your partner is cornering him on 52nd?"
Lieutenant Fish, *Barney Miller*

"Eeeh, is you is or is you ain't my baby?"
Bugs Bunny, *Bugs Bunny*

"Does your mother know what you do for a living?"
Jim Rockford, *The Rockford Files*

"Why do they call it *rush hour* when nothing moves?"
Mork, *Mork and Mindy*

"Why do they call them *tellers?* They never tell you anything. They just ask questions. And why do they call it *interest?* It's boring."
Coach Ernie Pantusso, *Cheers*

Mom, do you ever get that not-so-fresh feeling?
Summer's Eve commercial

"Question numero uno, Jorge, Graciella. ¿Quien es mas macho—Fernando Lamas o Ricardo Montalban? ¿Fernando Lamas o Montalban?"
Paco, *Saturday Night Live*

CHRISSY: I have a two-part question—why?
JACK: How's that a two-part question?
CHRISSY: We both want to know.
Three's Company

"Did I ever tell you about my Uncle Bernie who never took a bath?"
Gabe Kotter, *Welcome Back, Kotter*

"Can I go outside and play, Paw?"
Opie Taylor, *The Andy Griffith Show*

"Oh, Boss, she's beautiful. Who is she?"
Tattoo, *Fantasy Island*

"Would you like to sit down, hairball, or do you prefer internal bleeding?"
Mick Belker, *Hill Street Blues*

"Perhaps we should ask ourselves, Natasha, is it worth all the effort? Is a cheesy, million-dollar treasure worth getting blown up for? Is a million dollars really that important? Is money everything? . . . You bet it is! Get back to work!"
Boris, *Rocky and Bullwinkle*

Normisms

Everyone knows his name. Every day (or was it night?) he'd come through the door and saunter to his stool—the closest point to the beer and the bathroom. Beer was his life, and he loved it.

He was Norm, and from 1982 to 1992, everyone at *Cheers* knew him. Here are some of Norm's best-known entrance lines.

COACH: How's life treating you, Norm?
NORM: Like it caught me in bed with his wife.

COACH: How about a beer, Norm?
NORM: Hey, I'm high on life, Coach. Of course, beer is my life.

COACH: How's a beer sound, Norm?
NORM: I dunno. I usually finish them before they get a word in.

COACH: What's shaking, Norm?
NORM: All four cheeks and a couple of chins, Coach.

COACH: What would you say to a nice beer, Normie?
NORM: Going down?

WOODY: What can I do for you, Mr. Peterson?
NORM: Elope with my wife.

WOODY: Hey, Mr. Peterson, Jack Frost nipping at your nose?
NORM: Yep, now let's get Joe Beer nipping at my liver, huh?

"How can you stay with a woman who tried to kill you?"
Matt, *Melrose Place*

Q: How many Martians does it take to screw in a lightbulb?
A: 8.2
Mork, *Mork and Mindy*

"May I have a glass of water?"
Cindy Loo Who, *The Grinch Who Stole Christmas*

The "To Be or Not To Be" Song, from GILLIGAN'S ISLAND

Perhaps no other episode of *Gilligan's Island* (1964–1967 on CBS) is more beloved than the one in which Phil Silvers, a big Broadway producer, somehow ends up on the island and the castaways try to convince him to take them back with him by putting on a musical version of *Hamlet*.

True to form, the crew of the *Minnow* remains lost—Phil decides to steal the idea and stage his own version of the musical, leaving the islanders stranded again.

Here are some of the words Gilligan brought to life in his unforgettable performance, the now-famous "To Be or Not To Be" speech, to be sung to the tune of "The Habañera" from *Carmen*.

I ask to be,
Or not to be
A rogue or a peasant slave is what you see.
A boy who loved
His mother's knee
And so I ask to be or not to be.
So hear my plea,
I beg of thee
And say you see a little hope for me.
To fight or flee,
To fight or flee,
I ask myself to be or not to be.

"Which way to the batroom?"
Batman, *Batman*

Poetry

"Calling Dr. Bombay! Calling Dr. Bombay!
Emergency! Emergency! Come right away!"
Samantha, *Bewitched*

Aaron Spelling Bee

More than a king.
More than a messiah.
More than a prophet.
There is no word that describes Aaron Spelling and his contribution to our lives. Just as it is imp
to know the Ten Commandments by heart, and, to know the sutras of Buddha by soul, it is vital to
the canon of Spelling. And how to spell them.

1. This show featured a husband-and-wife team of crime-fighting, justice seekers. They were to
They were clever. They were in love . . .
   H-A-R-T T-O H-A-R-T

2. Hip, undercover cops, in Los Angeles.
   M-O-D S-Q-U-A-D

3. How do you spell one of many prime-time soap operas featuring the twisted and incestuous
dealings of a family whose lives resembled a continuous wartime saga?
   D-Y-N-A-S-T-Y

4. How do you spell the family name?
   C-A-R-R-I-N-G-T-O-N

5. The first of the Saturday night powerhouse shows.
   L-O-V-E B-O-A-T

6. The second of the Saturday night powerhouse shows.
   F-A-N-T-A-S-Y I-S-L-A-N-D

7. Spell the best of the giggle shows, and the three primary gigglers.
   C-H-A-R-L-I-E-'S A-N-G-E-L-S
   S-A-B-R-I-N-A D-U-N-C-A-N
   J-I-L-L M-U-N-R-O-E
   K-E-L-L-Y G-A-R-R-E-T-T

If in heaven we don't meet
Hand in hand we'll bear the heat.
And if ever it gets too hot,
Pepsi-Cola
Hits the spot.
> **What Shirley wrote in Laverne's yearbook,** *Laverne and Shirley*

Why, hello there, Miss Jones! You sure got nice—bones!
> ***Sesame Street***

"There was a young lady from Venus
Whose body was shaped like a . . . "
> **Data,** *Star Trek: The Next Generation*

8. Although it was odd to see the star of this show go from futuristic space to being a cop in LA. we accepted it. Probably because he was such a talented fighter.
T.-J. H-O-O-K-E-R

9. A spin-off of number 3. Different family, same problems.
T-H-E C-O-L-B-Y-S

10. Number 5 moves into port and deals with the same cosmic questions using a different crew.
H-O-T-E-L

11. The Waltons move to Pasadena, circa the 70s.
F-A-M-I-L-Y

12. Two-word clue: Grand Tourismo.
S-T-A-R-S-K-Y A-N-D H-U-T-C-H

13.Husband-and-wife cop team who kept their identities under cover in the 80s.
M-A-G-R-U-D-E-R A-N-D L-O-U-D

14. Beating, cop team action.
S-W-A-T

15. To this day, in airports around the world, the arrival and departure monitors spell this destination the way it was spelled on Spellingvision.
V-E-G-A-$

16. The present-day teen soap we love to hate cause they're too cool and too rich. Hint: Proof that nepotism is alive and well.
B-E-V-E-R-L-Y H-I-L-L-S 9-0-2-1-0

17. The other one
M-E-L-R-O-S-E P-L-A-C-E

"Oh my darlin'
Oh my darlin'
Oh my daaaaaarlin'
Whats'er name . . ."
Huckleberry Hound

"Each fella for all and all for each fella.
Our loyalty never quits.
Everyone knows bananas are yella',
But not the Banana Splits!
Hey, hey, hey!"
Banana Splits

Imponderables from the Television Universe

Here are the unanswerable questions from the TV universe, questions with which millions of couch potatoes have struggled over the years.

These topics are appropriately raised at social gatherings, at family events, in bars—anywhere good discussions take place and where TV and truth rule.

If Colonel John "Hannibal" Smith, B.A. Barracus, Templeton "Face" Peck, and H.M. "Howlin' Mad" Murdock made up the A-Team, who made up the B-Team?

☐ Did Mel ever kiss Flo's grits?

☐ Would Archie Bunker have been so mean to Meathead if he knew he would some day be a big-shot Hollywood director?

☐ When Buck Rogers was frozen into the 25th century, why did everybody have the same bad 1980s haircuts when he got there?

☐ Which one was Cagney and which one was Lacey?

☐ What kind of benefits did Charlie offer his Angels? Did he have a 401K plan?

☐ Were Daisy and Luke Duke kissing cousins?

☐ Who got surveyed for the questions on *Family Feud*?

☐ Was Mr. Roarke God?

☐ Why was one *Price Is Right* showcase always so much better than the other?

☐ How did Oscar Madison go from being such a slob one season to knowing all that stuff about dead people the next?

☐ What was really in a Scooby snack?

☐ Were Ernie and Bert gay?

☐ What's Steve Austin's blue-book value today?

☐ How did Spiderman know when his Spider sense was tingling or when he just really had to pee?

☐ How come the *Star Trek* crew didn't have seatbelts?

☐ Was *Superfriends* based on real events?

☐ Did Rusty ever have to pull his gun to settle a dispute in *The People's Court*?

☐ Did Jim and Stan ever sit back in the bushes and let Marlin Perkins do the wrestling?

☐ How did Wonder Woman turn *back* into Diana Prince?

☐ Did Shirley Feeney ever put out for Carmine?

☐ How come Andy Griffith never went to visit his old deputy, Mr. Furley, when he lived below Jack, Janet, and Chrissy?

"Durwood, I do not like the way you gloat,
So I'm turning you into a billy goat."
Endora, *Bewitched*

IT BEATS BURYING YOURSELF
IN THE SAND:
LOVE, SEX, AND MARRIAGE

Some cultures consider it necessary to have a wife and a girlfriend. Others consider it a sin. In some cultures, women have the freedom to choose who they will marry, if they do. In other cultures, marriages are arranged, and love is less of a consideration. In Greece, when a husband and wife are heard fighting, the eavesdropper thinks, "How wonderful. They are making love."

When it comes to love, sex, and marriage, everyone has their own ideas, and some of our best and worst examples of how to have a loving relationship come from TV. Television shows us the extremes—passionate marriages as seen on *Hart to Hart*, torrid affairs as seen on *Dynasty, Melrose Place*, and other Spelling shows, tumultuous relationships as seen on *All in the Family*.

These are all lessons that we can take to heart, when it comes to matters of the heart.

● ● ● ● ● ● ● ● ● ● ● ● ● ● ● ● ● ●

"Love does not ask to see your I.D."
    Keith Partridge, *The Partridge Family*

"Love hurts."
    Kimberly, *Melrose Place*

"Wookin' pa nub in all da wong paces."
    Buckwheat, *Saturday Night Live*

How to Set Up a Blind Date Like Chuck Woolery on *THE LOVE CONNECTION*

Chuck Woolery. The Man. The Myth. The Yenta. Starting in 1983, Chuck—the smoothy—made love connections. Sometimes the couples made it, sometimes the connection shorted out. Whatever the outcome, it was always fun to "go along" on the date. Now you can try it with your friends. Here's how to set up your own *Love Connection*.

You will need:

- ☐ a group of friends to be the voting audience
- ☐ two couches
- ☐ a video camera in another room
- ☐ a large screen to play that video back

1. Find a woman who has strict rules about the men she wants to date. Some guidlines are:

I will date a man with brains.
I will date a man with a butt.
I will not date a man with b.o.
I will not date a man with bell bottoms.
I will not date a man with bad breath.

2. Find three men who all have horror stories about dating. Be sure they have integrated these mistakes into the standards of the women they date. If you can't find ones with standards, find one sensitive guy, one macho guy, and one geek.

"I once went to the beach with this babe and she was pulling out her compact all the time and fixing her hair . . . and you're at the beach you know, so just let it down and have a good time."

"I had this date with a girl and she was nice enough and I thought she was the right one, until at the end of the date, I called her by the name of the girl I had gone

---

MINDY: You can't fight *hate* with *hate*. I was always taught to fight *hate* with *love* and *understanding*.
MORK: That's 2 to 1. Pretty good odds.
   Mork and Mindy

"If Marilyn's clock of romance has finally started to tick, it would not behoove us to overwind her mainspring."
   Herman Munster, *The Munsters*

"I've got to round up a couple of girls and try to persuade them that the man in their stars is short, dark, and handsome . . . hmm . . . bye-bye, Boss."
   Tattoo, *Fantasy Island*

"It's hard enough to meet a woman you dislike, much less like."
   George, *Seinfeld*

out with the night before . . . and, well, that was a mistake."

"I like women who want to be mothers. You know, the nurturing type who are looking for something more than singles bars and dating games."

3. Sit on the couch opposite the woman and play the videotaped segments of the guys.

4. Have the audience scream out which bachelor they think she should date. Be sure they hold their hands up in the air with the number of fingers showing as they scream.

5. Ask the woman to pick one of the men, and go out on a date with him.

6. One month later, gather the men, woman, and audience together to hear about the date. Be sure that the man she picked is there, in another room but visible on the screen. Ask about the intimate details of the date. Make faces at words like, *hot, heavy, wet,* and *hard* regardless of what they're talking about. For example:

So we went down to the pool area, and the walkway was kind of wet.
(Make a face.)
And then we went on this hike up a mountain and it was fun, but really hard.
(Raise your eyebrows.)

7. If the date worked out and both of them liked each other, take a poll of the audience's original vote. If the audience voted for someone else, say:

"Aw, too bad, but I guess you two will be going out again, huh?"
If the audience voted for him, say:

"Well, great, so I guess we made a Love Connection here! If you two want to go out again we'll pay for it."

If the date didn't work out, see who the audience voted for and send them out on another date.

8. Say, "We'll be back in two and two" and then cut to a commercial.

JAIME SOMERS: What kind of a life are we gonna have with each other?
STEVE AUSTIN: What kind of a life are we gonna have without each other?
The Six Million Dollar Man

"Marriage is totally essential. Why, without marriage, husbands and wives would have to fight with total strangers."
Grandpa Jones, *Hee Haw*

"Without infidelity, there would be no *Dynasty,* no *Divorce Court,* no Ann Landers."
David Addison, *Moonlighting*

"Fighting is what keeps a marriage together."
Roseanne Connor, *Roseanne*

"Just 'cause I said 'yes' when we got married don't mean I gotta keep sayin' 'yes' all the rest of my life."
Edith Bunker, *All in the Family"*

I happen to believe in the sanctity of marriage—no matter how ugly or disgusting it gets."
Frank Burns, *M*A*S*H*

"Last week, your mother wished to marry the man she loved . . . today, you ask me to kill the man."
Caine, *Kung Fu*

"A wife. Why not? It sure beats burying yourself in the sand."
Grandpa Munster, *The Munsters*

"Alfred, at the risk of sounding pompous, experience with women and experience with wives are two very different things."
Commissioner Gordon, *Batman*

"Before all that equality crapola, you was a sweet, frightened wife."
Archie Bunker, *All in the Family*

PROFESSOR: Kissing on the mouth is far from sanitary. It can lead to all sorts of bacterial transfer.
GINGER: You certainly make a kiss sound romantic. Like some sort of germ warfare.
Gilligan's Island

PRIVATE INVESTIGATOR: I'm looking for a young woman.
GOPHER: Who isn't?
The Love Boat

"We were gonna dedicate this whole month to meeting new girls!"
Oscar Madison, *The Odd Couple*

How to Have a Relationship on
THE LOVE BOAT

Our parents grew up thinking that life was a musical—that they would sing and dance their way through life with their true loves. We grew up thinking that life was like the Love Boat—that we would grow up and sail off to Puerta Vallarta with our true loves. We still can; here's how. You'll need to start with at least six friends, preferably dressed in white shorts.

IF YOU ARE SINGLE

- ☐ Board the ship after a breakup.
- ☐ Meet that flame, old or new, in a passageway or preferably on the Shuffleboard Deck.
- ☐ Argue over who loves the other more.
- ☐ Talk to a crew member about true happiness.
- ☐ Meet on the Promenade Deck to the light of a fake moon, and be together forever.

IF YOU ARE A COUPLE

- ☐ Board the ship to rekindle that spark.
- ☐ Meet each other on the Lido Deck after dinner.
- ☐ Argue over something in the past. "You never listen, you're always paying attention to other people," etc.
- ☐ Talk to a crew member about misery.
- ☐ Meet on the Promenade Deck to the light of a fake moon, and be together forever.

FLOYD: This is how it happens . . . she'll want to come over to your house to make supper. And then she'll take Opie upstairs and tuck him into bed. And then she'll offer to come the next day. And the next day. And then she'll kinda hint around that she wants to do this all the time. And then it happens . . .

ANDY: What happens?

FLOYD: You'll be out changing the card on your mailbox to read . . . Mr. and Mrs. Andy Taylor.
   The Andy Griffith Show

"Devon, if I meet a young woman I want her to whisper sweet nothings into my ear, not crises involving military hardware . . ."
   Michael Knight, *Knight Rider*

FLO: Hi handsome, what would you like?

CUSTOMER: Well, what have you got in mind?

FLO: If it's the same thing you have in mind, you ain't gonna find it on the menu.

Alice

"It's a male strip joint! We could see things there that could trigger hormones we never knew we had."

Natalie, *Facts of Life*

MICHAEL: You decent?

AMANDA: That's a matter of opinion.

Melrose Place

JEANNIE: Are you content, Master?

MAJOR NELSON: Well, who wouldn't be? A lovely girl like you, a deserted island . . . oh, and this wine looks nice, too.

I Dream of Jeannie

GRIEVING WIDOW: Do you know what it's like to be married to a wonderful man for fourteen years?

LT. FRANK DREBIN: No, I can't say that I do. I did . . . uh . . . live with a guy once, though, but that was just for a couple of years. The usual slurs, rumors, innuendos—people just didn't understand.

Police Squad

"Mr. Roarke, let me tell you something . . . I have never, in my life, been able to say the words *I love you*."

Sammy Davis, Jr., *Fantasy Island*

"That's the funny thing about people and animals. If you love 'em enough to let 'em go, they love ya' enough to come back."

Girl and James Adams, *Grizzly Adams*

"It's fate. . . . Marriages is made in Tennessee."

Granny Clampitt, *The Beverly Hillbillies*

RALPH MALPH: I got all twelve issues of
National Geographic magazine.

POTSIE WEBER: Nude Pygmies!

Happy Days

"Every time I see him on TV, I think, Wow! Desi Arnaz, Jr. . . . he's so cute! In my dream of dreams, I dream of being Mrs. Desi Arnaz, Jr.!"

Marcia Brady, *The Brady Bunch*

Geoff: I haven't touched a woman since I met you.

KIRBY: And I haven't touched a man who mattered . . . since you.

Dynasty

JENNIFER: Do you want me to pick his pocket?

JONATHAN: I'd prefer it if you didn't get that close to him.

Hart to Hart

"Take it from me, there's only one way to get over a woman. Find another one."

Vinnie Barbarino, *Welcome Back, Kotter*

"You fall head over heels, you don't always land on your feet."
Gopher, *The Love Boat*

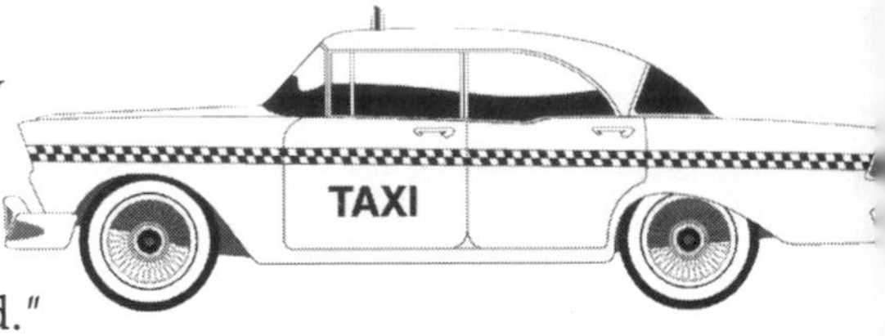

"Simka, I have learned my
lesson. I think you are a
wonderful person and I am
proud to be the man whose
life you have totally wrecked."
Latka, *Taxi*

"So, I'm just another lymphoma to you?"
Amanda, *Melrose Place*

SUZANNA: Are you gonna call me, or am I supposed to call you?
GARY: Yes.
ThirtySomething

"Nice legs . . . for a human."
Worf, *Star Trek: The Next Generation*

DARRIN: Al, my wife is a witch.
BARTENDER: Cheer up, you should see my wife.
Bewitched

I AM YOUR FATHER. I BROUGHT YOU INTO THIS WORLD, AND I CAN TAKE YOU OUT: RELATIONSHIPS AMONG FAMILY AND FRIENDS, MEN AND WOMEN

What in life matters more than family and friends? What is more important than spending holidays with your loved ones, the ones who know you best, support and nourish you, or at least, can annoy you more than anyone else in the world?

Nothing—unless it's sitting at home alone, watching a good television show that gets you thinking about your life's relationships instead of actually experiencing them.

This chapter is devoted to the most important relationships of all—the ones on *Three's Company, ThirtySomething, The Cosby Show,* and *Alice.* They did, after all, teach us to get along with one another.

●●●●●●●●●●●●●●●●●

"I am your father. I brought you into this world—and I can take you out."
    Cliff Huxtable, *The Cosby Show*

"I don't wanna be alone with my mother. I have never wanted to be alone with my mother."
    Ellen, *ThirtySomething*

"I even think you're groovy—for a sister, that is."
Greg Brady, *The Brady Bunch*

RUDY: Daddy, do Grandma and Grandpa know
   how to take care of little kids?
CLIFF: Well, sure they do, they brought me up. And
   how do you think I turned out?
RUDY: Tall.
   The Cosby Show

"Well, now isn't this nice? In the home of my *wonderful* son, and
my *handsome* grandson . . . and my daughter-in-law."
Mother Jefferson, *The Jeffersons*

JESSICA: Hi, Daddy.
COLONEL: You know, I'll never be able to understand why you
   think I'm your father.
   Soap

"My wife will be home soon. Can you say, 'bitch?' . . . That's
our special word today. Walk into Momma's room and say
'bitch!' Did she slap you? Then you did it right!"
   Mr. Robinson, *"Mr. Robinson's Neighborhood" Saturday
   Night Live*

Friends

JULIE MCCOY: Why don't you come inside? I'll make you a Julie
   McCoy special.
ISAAC: What's that?
JULIE: It's a tall glass of tonic with a healthy shot of tender loving
   care.
   The Love Boat

"Not minding—that's what friends are for!"
   Ernie, *Sesame Street*

"I like you just the way you are."
   Mister Rogers' Neighborhood

"I feel like Charlie and I've got my Angels back."
   Mel Sharpels, *Alice*

"Just remember—friends do it, too."
Brittany Maddocks, *Melrose Place*

"If you can't betray your friends, who can you betray?!"
Downtown Brown, *Simon and Simon*

Men and Women

"You know, boys, a nuclear reactor is a lot like a woman. You just have to read the manual and press the right buttons."
Homer Simpson, *The Simpsons*

"If you had what other men have, I wouldn't need batteries."
Peg Bundy, *Married with Children*

"Men have menopause, too. They just haven't had all the bad press we women have."
Maude Finlay, *Maude*

"If women are so smart, why do they dance backwards?"
Steve McGarrett, *Hawaii Five-0*

"Men can sit through the most pointless, boring movie if there's even the slightest possibility that a woman will take her top off."
Elaine, *Seinfeld*

"He is just a man, and I am Erica Kane. Need I say more?"
Erica Kane, *All My Children*

"You gotta act gentle and polite to a woman-type female."
Magilla Gorilla, *Magilla Gorilla*

"You can make a man eat shredded cardboard—if you know the right tricks."
Jeannie's Evil Sister, *I Dream of Jeannie*

"Women: Can't live with 'em, can't leave 'em on the curb when you're done with them."
David Addison, *Moonlighting*

The Evil Twin Yearbook

Ah, the Evil Twin episode—a classic plot twist that allows our hero or heroine to flex his or her acting muscles by playing a dual role. (It also serves the added benefit of saving the producers a lot of money they would have otherwise spent on a guest star.)

We've seen evil twins in *Knight Rider, Star Trek, I Dream of Jeannie, Bewitched,* and many other shows, and we've always wondered the same thing: What were they like growing up?

Now, we can find out. We've discovered the yearbook entries of several famous TV characters and their evil twins, and we reprint them here for your reading pleasure.

As you read, ask yourself this question—are you certain you know which one is evil?

MICHAEL KNIGHT

Member of debate team;
track team; community service club.
Most likely to go into public service, race car driving, or to become a lifeguard.
Motto: "One man can make a difference."

EVIL TWIN

Wood shop aide;
President of Anarchist's club;
Voted most likely to grow a bad goatee, harass others, and say evil things.
Motto: "Why me?"

CAPTAIN KIRK

Member of Boxing Club and
Leadership Club; student body president; captain of cheerleading squad; Singles Club.
Most likely to boldy go where no man has gone before.
Motto: "Beam me up."

EVIL CAPTAIN KIRK

Member of Fighting Dirty Club and Sexual Harrassment Club; captain of Brotherly Resentment Club.
Most likely to hang around outside convenience stores.
Motto: "Eat my shorts."

JEANNIE

Member of Home Economics Club, Fashion Club, and Dancers Anonymous. Most likely to settle down in a nice bottle.
Motto: "As you wish."

JEANNIE'S EVIL SISTER

Member of Daughters of Baghdadian Genies Association and Master Stealers Anonymous.
Most likely to expose her navel.
Motto: "You asked for it."

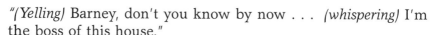

"(Yelling) Barney, don't you know by now . . . (whispering) I'm the boss of this house."
Fred Flintstone, *Flintstones*

"I think we'll have a wonderful time, just us girls."
Kip, *Bosom Buddies*

"My mother would rather I date a pig than a mountain girl."
Latka, *Taxi*

ALICE

Member of Housecleaners Associaton; bake sale organizer; Bad Jokers Anonymous.
Most likely to become ninth wheel to a large family of boys and girls.
Motto: "You're the boss."

SAMANTHA

Member of WTA (Witch's/Teacher's Association), captain of Spirit Squad, Mother Haters Anonymous.
Most likely to wrinkle her nose and change the course of history.
Motto: "Oh, Mother!"

JULIE McCOY

Member of GPA (Girls for a Perkier America), shuffleboard team, Spanish Club (organized trips to Puerta Vallarta).
Most likely to organize fun and exciting cruise ship events, like dancing on the Lido Deck and parasailing.
Motto: "Come aboard! We're expecting you."

COUSIN EMMA

Member of Motorcycle Club; Tattooists Anonymous; president of the Apathy Club.
Most likely to drive an eighteen wheeler, drink too much coffee, and remain alone.
Motto: "Out of the way."

SERENA

Member of Bad Hair Club for Witches, president of Home Wreckonomics Club, Husband Stealers Anonymous.
Most likely to wear tight skirts and dance the hoosgow while levitating.
Motto: "You mother#@$&!"

JUDY McCOY

Member of GOR (Girls on the Rebound) support group, Welcome Wagon, Pep Club Haters Anonymous. Most likely to join a successful TV show in it's waning years, becoming a shallow replacement for her cousin Julie.
Motto: "At least I don't have a coke habit."

GREG: What would you do if you had two dates for the same night? See, I don't want either girl to get hurt.
ALICE: Why don't you tell 'em both the truth?
GREG: The truth? Why tell a girl the truth?
   The Brady Bunch

"Pushy is the way it's done, Felix. It's custom all over the world. Man pursues Woman. Except for a few Polynesian islands and some bars in Greenwich Village."
   Oscar Madison, *The Odd Couple*

How to Misunderstand Your Friends, According to THREE'S COMPANY

Without a doubt one of the worst (and yet most successful) shows of the late 70s and early 80s, *Three's Company* was also one of the least original shows in terms of its plots. Based upon the British comedy *A Man About the House*, it portrayed the antics of three roommates, Jack Tripper (John Ritter), Janet Wood (Joyce DeWitt), and Chrissy Snow (Suzanne Somers). Tripper played a heterosexual caterer who pretended to be gay so that the landlord Mr. Roper (the best performance in the series, by Norman Fell) would allow him to live with two women. It ran from 1977 through 1984 and inflicted two painful spinoffs upon us—*The Ropers* and *Three's a Crowd*.

The truly remarkable thing about this show was that its plotline was virtually the same week to week: Someone mishears something the other person says, and it causes problems. Here's a handy guide to having similiar communication difficulties with your own friends.

1. Walk unannounced into rooms. Enter quietly, so that if someone else is in there they don't see you right away.
2. Try to overhear only the ends of conversations.
3. Make a practice of seeing your friends outside of your apartment—say, at the Regal Beagle. Don't let them see you.
4. When in doubt, assume the worst.
5. Sneak visitors into your bedroom late at night. Your roommates will have done the same thing. This will allow you to act strange the next morning, thus encouraging misinterpretation and poor communication.
6. When you are finally confronted (or confront others) with the misunderstanding, laugh shake your head, and say:
   a. Oh, Janet.
   b. Oh, Jack.
   c. Oh, Chrissy. You know I love you.
      Hug and make up.
7. Head back to the Regel Beagle to meet Larry for a celebration.
8. Leave Mr. Roper, who was listening at the door, totally confused.

BULLWINKLE: I'm your man!
BORIS: Moose!
BULLWINKLE: Moose!
Rocky and Bullwinkle

"Behind every successful man, there's a woman with a big mouth."
Rob Petrie, *The Dick Van Dyke Show*

"He wasn't any good. Handsome men never are."
Store Owner, *Dragnet*

"We get guys like that in here all the time . . . really unmellow."
Henchwoman, *Wonder Woman*

IT'S BETTER TO LOOK GOOD THAN TO FEEL GOOD: LOOKS, INTELLIGENCE, AND FEELINGS

*B*eauty takes many forms—a beautiful face, a beautiful mind, a beautiful heart. Some see beauty from the outside, others from the inside. But whatever your point of view, beauty is a standard that is either met, altered, or looked past.

Intelligence is also subjective. Some may have earned their intelligence from books, others from years at sea. The academic might not fare well on the ocean, and the sailor might not fare well in the classroom, but neither is necessarily more intelligent.

Feelings can be irrational. Feelings can be anticipated. Feelings can be fulfilling. They guide us closer to ourselves and moments of happiness, and they can take us away from our "charted" mental goals. Feelings can open our minds, and they can frighten our hearts.

Our TV friends both reflect our standards of beauty and dictate them. Nancy Drew chased the clues and put them together into working theories, while Squiggy "Squiggman," even in his lovable stupidity, always came through for his friends. *Seinfeld's* George does battle with his limiting emotions, while Spock feels nothing at all.

● ● ● ● ● ● ● ● ● ● ● ● ● ● ● ● ●

"You know what makes this country great? You don't have to be witty or clever as long as you can hire someone who is."
Ted Baxter, *The Mary Tyler Moore Show*

How to Pose Like CHARLIE'S ANGELS

Between 1976 and 1981 an amazing thing happened to TV crime fighting—it became a lot more attractive.

Here are our instructions for posing like the Angels did, in the classic commercial transition silhouette.

1. Get two friends.

2. Decide who will be Jill (or Kris), Sabrina, and Kelly.

3. Stand close together.

4. The following poses should all be struck simultaneously.

   a. Jill should bend forward at the waist and at both knees, with one leg extended as if she were about to step into action. With her right hand she should hold and aim a handgun. With her left arm she should support her right wrist. Her hair should be flowing.

   b. Kelly should bend forward at the waist and at both knees, with one leg extended as if she were about to jump into action.

   Note: *This body position should mirror Jill's. Her left and right arms should be extended with right arm slightly higher but aligned with her left. Both hands should be extended out in full kung-fu position.*

   c. Sabrina should stand in the middle, facing Jill with her right arm on her hip and her left holding a walkie-talkie to her mouth. (Pretend you are talking to Charlie.)

5. Once each of you has studied and practiced getting into these positions and feel comfortable enough to jump directly into them, find a friend who can play the "Incidental Cut to a Commercial *Charlie's Angels* Theme." (DUH-duh, DUH-duh, DAH-DAH . . . DADADADADADADADA!)

6. Play the music.

7. Jump into position.

Congratulations, Angels! You've done it again!

"You American girls have such big breasts all the time."
   The "Czechoslovakian Swinger" (Dan Akroyd),
      Saturday Night Live

Mrs. Howell: Are you absolutely certain that we're going to be captured by the cannibals, Thurston?
Mr. Howell: Yes, my dear, it's terribly distressing. I just don't know what to wear to a capture.
   Gilligan's Island

How to Deal with Anger, According to
THE INCREDIBLE HULK

Bruce Banner (played by Bill Bixby) was not a happy camper from 1978 to 1982. Not only was he a scientist who hadn't really made any major discoveries or won any significant awards, but he was accidentally exposed to gamma radiation, to boot. As a result, Banner became Lou Ferrigno in green makeup.

The Incredible Hulk was a precursor to the Men's Movement that came to fruition in the early 90s. Scientist Bruce Banner, played by Bill Bixby, was mild-mannered, helpful, and kind—but within him lurked the Hulk, the fierce, dark, green side of everyman. These were the waning Alan Alda days of sensitive new-age guys, and men were starting to get back in touch with their wild natures. *The Incredible Hulk* was one of the first shows to explore this side of manhood.

From *The Incredible Hulk* we learned a great many things, a few of which follow:

1. Don't get angry at every little thing. If you stub your toe, or break one of the good dishes while making dinner, just count to ten, take a deep breath, and move on.

2. When flying, try to get to the airport at least one and a half hours before the flight.

3. Avoid travelling during rush hour.

4. Put a small hook near the front door and get into the routine of hanging your keys on it as soon as you come home so that you don't lose them.

5. Don't watch any Judd Nelson films.

6. If you do feel yourself getting angry, try to go somewhere private. Move any breakable objects, like lamps, knick-knacks, and Volkswagen Beetles.

7. Buy cheap pants—preferably in colors that go well with green.

8. Keep an extra shirt with you at all times.

9. Grow accustomed to having to leave town quickly.

SKIPPER: I'm not overweight, I just have big bones.
GILLIGAN: Yeah, and they're covered with big meat.
    Gilligan's Island

"We have to have some weapons—besides our wits and good looks."
    Nancy Drew, *The Hardy Boys/Nancy Drew Mystery Show*

How to Interrogate Like COLUMBO

From 1971–1978, the detective named Columbo (Peter Falk) was perhaps the first of the Buddhist police detectives. We can all learn a lot from his Socratic techniques. Here are Columbo's rules. Try them on friends—you'll annoy them so much, they'll admit to anything.

1. Take an interest in the life of whomever you are questioning and find a way to tie it into your investigation. For example, if you are questioning a professor, go to his or her lecture, and question him or her after: "That pyramid stuff really interests me . . . the idea of burying a body where nobody will find it."

2. Be helpful. When approaching a suspect on the street, you could say, "Can I help you with your bags?"

3. Never let them make an excuse to get out of questioning:

THEM: Will this be quick? I haven't had dinner yet.

YOU: Oh. Neither have I. . . .Can I offer you some raisins?

4. Ask questions as if you know the answers, whether you do or not.

5. Be sure to give control to the interviewee. Let them think you are a pushover. Let them underestimate you: "I don't mean to interfere with your day, I'll let you go . . . oh, there's just one more thing."

6. Persistence. It is important to keep popping up at various times and various places in your suspect's life. This throws them off balance. This is the most effective method to get information if you don't really have any.

7. When it comes time to make the arrest, simply put the facts on the table. Let the criminals capture themselves. And most importantly, when you do get them, by all means, be humble. Light a cigar, smile to yourself, and think, "Oh, this nutty world."

SERGEANT FLINT: What'd you do? Take stupid lessons?
HONG KONG PHOOEY: No sir! I guess it just come to me natural!
Hong Kong Phooey

How to Outsmart Elmer Fudd, According to Bugs Bunny and Daffy Duck

The world is full of predators—greedy souls whose only purpose is to take advantage of everyone they meet; conquerors who believe the more they control, the happier they will be; hunters who devour the earth, without any regard for life—and Elmers who want to kill little fuwwy wabbits and smart-awec ducks, for no other reason than pure sport.

We've all been there—we've all been taken advantage of. This is the Bugs and Daffy method for turning the tables on the predators of the world.

YOUR CODE

1. **When You See a Trap, Jump Right In.** If someone wants to make a stew of you, don't run—hop in the pot and take a bath. If someone wants to trap you under a box, climb in and pull the top right down over you.

2. **Establish Trust.** When a gun is trained on you, walk right up to it and plug the barrel with your finger.

3. **Never Be Afraid to Cry.** If things are getting hairy and you're losing ground, give in. Cry and cower in fear as if you've been defeated. Then, when the Elmers let down a few of their defenses, move in.

Memorize the above standards. Get comfortable with them before you try any of the following.

STEP ONE: AGGRAVATION

1. Dazzle them with a song and dance.

2. Implicate your enemy. Grab a bear, hit him over the head with a log, hand the log to Elmer, run.

3. Let them take a potshot at you and then jump on their heads while they look for their victim.

STEP TWO: CONFUSION

1. Get behind the radio or TV and make an announcement that all rabbits or ducks are infected with highly contagious rabbititus or duckitus. Get close to Elmer until he runs away. Then, come knocking at the door dressed as a doctor, and convince him that he's sick.

Note: *Don't rush things. Convincing a healthy Elmer that he is sick can be fun. Enjoy it. Put him through the wringer.*

2. Use the Rabbit Season/Duck Season technique on page 113.

3. When being chased, stop. Turn around and seat your pursuer on a stadium seat. Hand them flags and caps and then work them into a cheering frenzy. Something like:

> Bric-a-brac-a
> Firecracker
> Sis boom bah!
> Bugs Bunny, Bugs Bunny
> Rah, rah, rah!

STEP THREE: DESTRUCTION

1. Dig a grave for yourself. Begin crying about your imminent demise, and as Elmer cries with you, shake his hand goodbye, turn him around, and slowly lower *him* into the grave.

2. Yell "Woo-hoo. Woo-hoo. W-hoo-hoo-hoo!" and hop away until the next time.

3. Give him a big, fat kiss on the mouth.

Final Note: If you find yourself at a loss at any moment, here are some quick-fix techniques for getting back on track:

☐ When burrowing or being chased under water, the split ears trick around a stump or a log works wonders.

☐ Put a lampshade on your head and switch yourself on.

☐ Convince him you have a wife and kids.

☐ One word—*hats*.

A.J. SIMON: What about amnesia? Have you ever had amnesia?
CLIENT: I don't remember.
Simon and Simon

"You know, my friends, it's better to look good than to feel good
. . . you know what I'm telling you."
Fernando, *Saturday Night Live*

"Pity's very underrated. I like pity. It's good."
George, *Seinfeld*

"You gotta give them city folks the benefit a' the doubt. It ain't
right to take advantage of them just 'cause they don't know any
better."
Uncle Jesse, *The Dukes of Hazzard*

How to Speak Ubbi Dubbi

Ubbi Dubbi was introduced to us by our friends at *Zoom* (1972–1979). Although many of us are able to do the "I'm Bernadette" arm twirl, even fewer have mastered Ubbi Dubbi—the secret language that identifies us to our other *Zoom*-watching brothers and sisters. We span the globe. We have no borders. We have no rulers. We have no tenses to conjugate. We are the Ubbi Dubbians. Here's a refresher course.

Take these phrases and practice Ubbi Dubbi. Find our brothers and sisters and reunite!

I	Ubbi
You	Yubbou
He, She, It	Hubbe, Shubbe, Ubbit
We	Wubbe
You (pl)	Yubbou
Them	Thubbem
Antidisestablishmentarianism	Ubbantubbidubbisubbestubbablubbish mubbentubbarubbianubbism
Hello	Hubbellubbo.
How are you?	Hubbow ubbare yubbou?
I am fine.	Ubbi ubbam fubbine.
The sweater is brown.	Thubbe swubbeatubber ubbis bruubbown.
Let it be, I am a monkey.	Lubbet ubbit bubbe, ubbi ubbam ubba mubbonkubbey.

For more information, write: *ZOOM*, Box 350, Boston, MA 02134

"Archie Bunker ain't no bigot. I'm the first to say, 'Look, it ain't your fault you're colored.'"
Archie Bunker,
All in the Family

PASSENGER: I used to live in New York City.
JUDY: Everyone makes mistakes.
The Love Boat

MR. SPOCK: A feeling is not much to go on.
KIRK: Sometimes a feeling, Mr. Spock, is all we humans have to go on.
Star Trek

"If only he had used his genius for niceness."
Maxwell Smart, *Get Smart*

"If ever we needed a brain, now is the time."
Squiggy, *Laverne and Shirley*

LIFE IS NOT ALL LOVELY THORNS AND SINGING VULTURES: THE REAL WORLD

*T*here are those of us who always swing at the everyday curveballs of life. There are those of us who let them fly by, taking a strike or a ball. We all know, deep down, that the balls will keep coming, and we can either take some joy from the pain life constantly dishes out, or we can wallow in limbo, in fear of taking the next step.

Rules help give us all a framework within which we can understand the world. Life's little joke is that as our understanding of the world grows, the rules change—like real-life channel-surfing.

This chapter brings to you a full array of perspectives on life—TV's take on the way life really is. Be free. Be well. And do the best you can.

● ● ● ● ● ● ● ● ● ● ● ● ● ● ● ● ● ●

"Having to be a free spirit twenty-four hours a day can be pretty exhausting . . . and pretty confusing."
Samantha, *Bewitched*

"Don't try this at home."
John Davidson, *That's Incredible!*

Don't squeeze the Charmin.
Charmin commercial

What to Worry About in Life, According to THIRTYSOMETHING

What will life be like when I grow up? What will we worry about? Luckily for us, we didn't have to worry about such things. We had Hope, Michael, Elliot, Nancy, Ellen, Gary, and Melissa, to show us. The *ThirtySomething* gang were the first of us to enter into real life. Here are some things to remember to worry about as you grow up.

☐ Who does the baby look like?

☐ Is this apartment good enough to be my last bachelor(ette) pad?

☐ Should I play the politics of the local college or leave all my friends in search of moral existence from an out-of-state teaching job?

☐ Should we celebrate Christmas or Hanukkah?

☐ Should I be the good child and take care of my mom's broken leg, or finally start my photography career with an assignment from *Vanity Fair*?

☐ Do I have an affair with the kindest person in the world or should I stay home in fear of the word *relationship* and order in?

☐ How *do* you spell *laxative*?

How to Join the Huxtable Men's Club

The Cosby Show ran from 1984–1992, and featured Cliff Huxtable, known for his sense of humor, good nature, bedside manner, and affinity for Philadelphia hoagies. Here are the rules to his Men's Club—join at your own risk.

1. No Women Allowed.
1. First, take roll call.
2. Throw out the nutritious food your wife left.
3. Whatever you eat is a secret.
4. If you can find a good woman, meeting adjourned.
5. If you can get rid of the other family members, you can have all the hoagies to yourself.
6. Eat the bad food.
7. No dancing girls.

"It's a dog-eat-dog world out there and I'm wearing Milkbone shorts."
Norm, *Cheers*

"Life is not all lovely thorns and singing vultures, you know."
Morticia, *The Addams Family*

"This is a cheap-shot comedy sketch, and I'll lay you odds the frog wrote it!"
Miss Piggy, *The Muppet Show*

"Wilderness sure does have a nice view. Not just the kind you can see, but the kind you can hear, too. 'Course, all the critters on the ground 'n in the air wanna be heard, too. Even the ones that don't have much of a voice."
Uncle Jack, *Grizzly Adams*

"Never make fun of a Ferengi's mother."
Ferengi Rule of Acquisition Number 31, *Deep Space Nine*

How to Use Conjunctions, According to SCHOOLHOUSE ROCK

Interjections were one thing, but conjunctions are another. Thankfully, we had *Schoolhouse Rock* to teach us about both of them.

CONJUNCTION JUNCTION

Conjunction Junction, what's your function?
Hookin' up words, and phrases, and clauses.
Conjunction Junction, how's that function?
I got three favorite cars that get most of my jobs done.
Conjunction Junction, what's their function?
I got AND, BUT, and OR—they'll get you pretty far.

Spoken:
AND—that's an additive, like this and that.
BUT—that's sort of the opposite, not this but that.
AND then there's OR, O-R, when you have a choice like this or that.
AND, BUT, and OR gets you pretty far!!!

Conjunction Junction, what's your function?
Hookin' up two boxcars and makin' them run right.
Milk n' Honey,
Bread n' Butter,
Peas n' Rice,
Hey that's nice!
Dirty but happy,
Diggin' and Scratchin',
Losin' your shoe and a button or two,
He's poor but honest,
Sad but true,
Boo hoo hoo hoo hoo.
Conjunction Junction, what's your function?
Hookin' up two cars to one when you say somethin' like this choice,

Spoken:
"Either now or later."
Or no choice,
"Neither now nor ever."
Hey that's clever.
Eat this or that.
Grow thin or fat.
Never mind—I wouldn't do that, I'm fat enough now!

Conjunction Junction, what's your function?
Hookin' up phrases and clauses that balance like:
Out of the frying pan, and into the fire.
He cut loose the sandbags but the balloon wouldn't go any higher.
Let's go up to the mountains or down to the seas.
You should always say thank you or at least say pleeeeeease.
Conjunction Junction, what's your function?
Hookin' up words and phrases and clauses and complex sentences like:

Spoken:
Conjunction Junction, what's your function?
Hookin' up cars and makin' them function.
Conjunction Junction, watch that function.
I'm gonna get you there, if you're very careful.
(repeat to fade)

How a Bill becomes a Law, According to SCHOOLHOUSE ROCK

And. of course, every self-respecting couch potato knows how the law works, thanks to *Schoolhouse Rock*.

I'M JUST A BILL

Spoken:

Woof! You sure gotta climb a lotta steps to get to this Capitol building here in Washington! But I wonder who that sad little scrap of paper is?

I'm just a bill,
Yes, I'm only a bill,
And I'm sitting here on Capitol Hill.
Well, it's a long, long journey
To the capital city,
It's a long, long wait
While I'm sitting in committee,
But I know I'll be a law someday.
At least I hope and pray that I will,
But today I'm still just a bill.

Spoken:

Gee, bill, you certainly have a lot ot patience and courage!

Well, I got this far. When I started, I wasn't even a bill. I was just an idea. Some folks back home decided they wanted a law passed, so they called their local congressman and he said, "You're right, there ought to be a law." Then he sat down and wrote me out and introduced me to Congress, and I became a bill. And I'll remain a bill until they decide to make me a law.

I'm just a bill.
Yes I'm only a bill,
And I got as far as Capitol Hill.
Well now I'm stuck in committe,
And I sit here and wait
While a few key congressmen
Discuss and debate
Whether they should
Let me be a law . . .
Oh, how I hope and pray that they will,
But today I am still just a bill.

Spoken:
Listen to those congressmen arguing! Most bills never even get this far. I hope they decide to report on me favorably, otherwise I may die.
Die?
Yeah: die in committee. Oooh! But it looks like I'm gonna live. Now I go to the House of Representatives and they vote on me.
If they vote "yes," what happens?
Then I go to the Senate and the whole thing starts all over again.
Oh, no!
Oh, yes!

I'm just a bill,
Yes, I'm only a bill.
And if they vote for me on Capitol Hill,
Well, then I'm off to the White House
Where I'll wait in a line
With a lot of other bills
For the President to sign.
And if he signs me then I'll be a law . . .
Oh, how I hope and pray that he will,
But today I am still just a bill.

Spoken:
You mean even if the whole Congress says you should be a law, the President can still say no?
Yes, that's called a "veto." If the President vetoes me, I have to go back to Congress, and they vote on me again, and by that time it's . . .
By that time, it's very unlikely that you'll become a law! It's not easy to become a law, is it?

No! But how I hope and I pray that I will,
But today I am still just a bill!

Spoken:
He signed you, bill! Now you're a law!
Oh, yes!

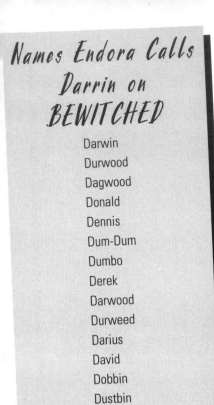

Names Endora Calls Darrin on *BEWITCHED*

Darwin

Durwood

Dagwood

Donald

Dennis

Dum-Dum

Dumbo

Derek

Darwood

Durweed

Darius

David

Dobbin

Dustbin

"Mom always said, 'Don't play ball in the house'."
Peter Brady, *The Brady Bunch*

"For a fugitive there are no freeways; all roads are toll roads to be paid in blood and pain."
Voice Over, *The Fugitive*

"If we don't say anything, at least we won't be lyin'."
Mary Ingalls, *Little House on the Prairie*

HERB: We've got a problem, Big Guy.
MR. CARLSON: Well, then solve it.
WKRP in Cinncinnati

"I'm alone in a world of weirdos."
Miss Piggy, *The Muppet Show*

"Some days you just can't get rid of a bomb."
Batman, *Batman*

"Jim, I thought it was dangerous enough just going down the face of that cliff. Let alone capturing a huge condor on the way."
Marlin Perkins, *Mutual of Omaha's Wild Kingdom*

Silly Rabbit! Trix are for kids!
Trix commercial

MAGGIE: I get the feeling this family isn't in the habit of going to church.
ARNOLD: We used to be in the habit, but we kicked it.
Diff'rent Strokes

10 Not-So-Good Reasons to Call
THE A-TEAM

Straight from the creative mind of Stephen J. Cannell (creator of such 80s powerhouse shows as the *Greatest American Hero, Hardcastle and McCormick,* and *Hunter*), *The A-Team* blasted onto viewers' screens in 1983. Until 1987, an unlikely team of Vietnam Veterans were at the beck and call of anyone who needed—and could afford—their help.

Featuring George Peppard as "Hannibal" Smith, Mr. T as D.A. Baracus, and Dirk Benedict fresh out of *Battlestar Galactica* as "Face" Peck, the tongue-in-cheek adventure show taught us all that help was always nearby. For staging military coups, foiling the mafia, and saving damsels in distress, no one in the mid-eighties was better prepared than the boys from *The A-Team.*

In their honor, here are ten not-so-good reasons to call for their assistance:

1. You can't find your keys.
2. There's something in your teeth.
3. You just want to talk.
4. The house is a mess.
5. You just don't feel fresh.
6. You're getting ready for a big date and you want to know if you "look okay."
7. You don't know whether to serve a white wine or a red wine.
8. Your regular sitter is busy.
9. "I can't reach that."
10. "My neck hurts right here . . ."

Meditation for Witches Who Do Too Much, by Samantha Stevens

Samantha in the 90s would most likely be part of the new-age healing movement. And she would likely have written her own book of affirmations and meditations. Here's a sample of the meditation that might have been.

Whoever is listening, be it my mother, Dr. Bombay, Uncle Arthur, Daddy, or some higher power, grant me the serenity to live my life on my own—the way I want to, with a mortal family and as a mortal wife. Let me raise my child on my own, with regular school and play, and no visits from dead historical characters and live teddy bears. Grant me the patience to forgive those who call my husband by the wrong names—MOTHER!—and who turn him into various farm animals or ruin his big advertising presentations. Allow me to make meals and clean house in my own way—if I don't want to zap up a dinner or twinkle the bathroom clean, it's O.K.—I'm just experiencing life. Love me for who I am, not for the magic that I do. And keep Aunt Esmerelda away as long as possible.

"It just goes to show you—it's always somethin'."
Roseanne Roseannadanna, *Saturday Night Live*

"You know, the very powerful and the very stupid have one thing in common, they don't alter their views to fit the facts, they alter the facts to fit the views, which can be uncomfortable, if you happen to be one of the facts that needs altering."
The Doctor, *Doctor Who*

"Oh, it's all my fault. I wanted to be an artist and now I've got a lot of statues and no friends."
Prickle, *Gumby*

HERMAN MUNSTER: Dancing's never been one of my strong
   points. I guess you could say I have two left feet.
GRANDPA MUNSTER: That's what happens when they put somebody together in the dark.
   The Munsters

Fonzie: Hey, like they say . . . to forgive is what?
RICHIE: Divine.
FONZIE: Diviiiiine.
   Happy Days

"The first thing to do when you're being stalked by an
angry mob with raspberries is to release a tiger."
   Instructor (John Cleese), *Monty Python's Flying
Circus*

"If the thraskin puts his fingers in his ears, it
is polite to shout."
   The Doctor, *Doctor Who*

"It is not the physical labor that challenges the
average man and woman; it is the constant assaults
on the spirit they must learn to endure. The vio-
lences against the soul are the ones that hurt the
most. The dreams that slip away into middle age;
the drudgery of the same job, year after year; the
day-to-day compromises; the boss who yells at
you; the waiter who looks down his nose because
you are wearing the wrong clothes. A thousand
tiny attacks that you and I never experience. Because
to try to become an average man is to try to become
one of the most overlooked, unappreciated, yet
noblest creatures of all."
   Mr. Roarke, *Fantasy Island*

DAMMIT, JIM, I'M A DOCTOR, NOT A BRICKLAYER: IDENTITY AND ACHIEVEMENT

*E*veryone, at one time or another, has an identity crisis: trying to figure out why they're here, what they've done with the last thirty years of their life, and what they'll do with the next thirty.

Luckily, we have our TV friends to keep us company along the way. We've been there for their crises, and most times we knew more about them than they knew about themselves.

But did Bones always want to be a doctor traveling the stars from the time he was a child? Was Bosley content to be the Angels' social director and act as the gravelly voiced liaison? Did Steve Austin ever want to turn away from a life of super-human strength?

Although most of our TV friends only had a half-hour a week to be, their identities shined through.

● ● ● ● ● ● ● ● ● ● ● ● ● ● ● ● ●

Identity

"We are more alike than unlike, my dear Captain. I have pores, humans have pores. I have fingerprints, humans have fingerprints. My chemical nutrients are like your blood. If you prick me, do I not . . . leak?"
    Data, *Star Trek: The Next Generation*

"Grasshopper, a man may tell himself many things. But is a man's universe made only of himself?"
    Master Po, *Kung Fu*

How to Deal with a Talent Scout You've Knocked Unconscious, According to Lucy

There are many different methods to use to get what you want when Ricky doesn't want you to even try. The best way involves learning to talk or trick your way into performing, and then winging it as the occasion demands. The nature of Lucy's schemes relied mainly on quick thinking. If you want to be like Lucy, you have to be able to do the same. Memorize this technique.

1. Get home and find a man who claims to be a talent scout in your apartment. Knock him out cold with a vase.

2. Answer the phone when Ricky calls and tells you that a talent scout is coming by to meet him. When you are questioned about your nervousness, just say you spilled some milk.

3. Clean up the vase and put the talent scout on the couch. He should still be unconscious, so prop him up and light him a cigarette.

4. When he comes to, be in the middle of a conversation with him: "You mean, you were saying that Elizabeth Taylor looks just as good off screen as she does on."

5. He should be well convinced that he had just blacked out; so when Ricky comes in, the talent scout will just carry on with his business.

Congratulations, you have just found out what part Ricky is up for and can plan an attack accordingly.

"Same old Cagney, huh? John Wayne in a skirt."
Captain Dorlan, *Cagney and Lacey*

"For the first seventeen years of my life I was my father's daughter. For the second seventeen I was my husband's wife. Now I have to find out who I am."
Ann Romano, *One Day at a Time*

"A woman's scent is her identity."
Linda Evans, *Forever Krystle commercial*

"Enterprising, socializing, everything but compromising— Maude!"
Maude **theme**

What Doctor McCoy Is Not, According to Himself

Whenever Doctor McCoy's in a situation that challenges his abilities, requires him to perform the seemingly impossible or falls outside his standard job description as chief medical officer of the *U.S.S. Enterprise,* Bones becomes stubborn, and passes the buck.

Suffice it to say that if McCoy were in the workforce today, he would not get very far with that attitude.

Dammit, Jim—I'm a doctor, not a bricklayer.
I'm a doctor, not a psychiatrist.
I'm a doctor, not a coal miner.
I'm a doctor, not a mechanic.
What am I, a doctor or a moon shuttle conductor?
I'm a doctor, not an escalator.
I'm a doctor, not an engineer.

"I'm disturbed, I'm depressed, I'm inadequate. I've got it all!"
George, *Seinfeld*

"I'm Mr. Heat Miser, I'm Mr. Sun."
Heat Miser, *The Year Without a Santa Claus*

CLAYTON: As your campaign manager . . . I made you.
BENSON: That'll come as a big surprise to my mother and father.
Benson

"I'm not out to win any popularity contests."
Erica Kane, *All My Children*

"Hey Jon, is there something wrong with the way I live? . . . I mean, you're never in trouble. And I always am."
Ponch, *CHiPs*

"I'm the captain of the ship of fools."
Captain Stubing, *The Love Boat*

"I suppose I'm to be left behind for the really heavy stuff . . . look after the office, answer the mail, pick up the phone when it rings."
Bosley, *Charlie's Angels*

"I'm a soldier, not a diplomat. I can only tell you the truth."
James T. Kirk, *Star Trek*

"I'm Gumby, dammit."
Gumby (Eddie Murphy), *Saturday Night Live*

"I'm a doctor, not a magician."
Dr. Pulaski, *Star Trek: The Next Generation*

How to Turn into WONDER WOMAN

One of the most important factors to remember if you have a secret identity is that no matter how much the real you and your super-hero look alike, no one will be able to tell who you really are. This makes changing into a super-hero much easier.

Diana Prince was in several high-speed chases during her years on the air with Steve Trevor from 1976–1979. She'd turn a corner ahead of him and use that moment to change. When he came running around the corner and saw her, he would say something like "Wonder Woman? Where's Diana?" She would respond with something like, "She's safe. Go and get the disk."

Now you can use the very method Diana Prince used to turn into Wonder Woman. Here's her four-step technique, in slo-mo.

1. Take off your huge, round glasses.

2. With your arms fully extended out, take a quarter-turn back for wind-up, hold, and release into a full three turns. The process here is simple.

When you begin your turn, a bright red and blue light should appear in front of you. If not, stop and take a deep breath, and try again. This may take some practice.

When the bright light surrounds you, this is your opportunity. Use the light as a cloak, as if a friend is holding a towel around you while you change your clothes on the beach.

3. Quickly stop turning and change into your selected Wonder Woman uniform.

Note: *This must happen quickly, as the light will only last a short time.*

When you are completely changed, go back into the turn and the light should fade all around. Do not get caught in the light.

The light should die out and you are revealed to the world as Wonder Woman.

4. And most importantly, be sure when you have completed the change to stop and look around. Take a moment to get your bearings again. Remember, there's nothing more embarrassing than a freshly changed Wonder Woman who trips and falls on her first steps to pursue the crooks because her equilibrium is off from all that turning.

5. Pursue and capture your criminals.

The "How Much of a Bitch Are You" Test, by Alexis Carrington and Sue Ellen Ewing

From 1978–1991 Sue Ellen Ewing put up with the good and the bad at the Mansion. From 1981–1989 Alexis Carrington had to face the trials and tribulations of the Denver-based millionaire family. Granted, both had to deal with a lot of life's garbage, but at their hearts, they were bitches.

Now you can measure your own ability to be a bitch. How do you compare to the pros? Did they teach you well?

1. When your ex-husband buys your firstborn from you in a moment of extreme weakness, you:
   a. Spend the rest of your life crying about it.
   b. Tell your ex that the child is an alien.
   c. Tell your ex that the child isn't his.
   d. Spend the rest of your life plotting to send the child to Burma to live with pygmies.

2. When your oil-mogul husband constantly sleeps around on you, you:
   a) Spend the rest of your life crying about it.
   b) Spend the rest of your life sleeping around on him.
   c) Force him to give you endless amounts of money.
   d) Shoot him with a small caliber handgun.

3. When your ex-husband's new wife tells you to stay out of his life, you:
   a) Spend the rest of your life crying about it.
   b) Spend the rest of your life trying to break them up.
   c) Grab her by the hair and pull her face down into your knee.
   d) Tell her, "Oh, darling, I wish you had told me that last night, I would have sent him home to you instead of doing him again."

4. If your banker tells you that you are virtually broke, you:
   a) Spend the rest of your life crying about it.
   b) Spend the rest of your life on credit.
   c) Tell your banker you know people who could take his bald head and turn it into a pumpkin if he doesn't carry you until your next deal goes through.
   d) Ask him what he's doing for dinner.

5. When a college friend of your son's, who just inherited millions of dollars, comes to you with an evil plan for a merger, you:
   a) Spend the rest of your life crying about the state of the world.
   b) Spend the rest of your life carrying about evil merger plans and pretending you don't know they're evil.
   c) Ask him how old he is and then take him on the desk.
   d) Turn him away and call him a little boy who'll be devoured if he thinks he can play with the wolves, and then go behind his back to make the merger happen without him.

Answer Key: "D" is always correct.
Scoring:
   1 Right—You're no bitch. Go back to Markie Post School.
   2 Right—You're merely irksome. Go back to Flo Castleberry School.
   3 Right—You're wicked, not bitchy. Go back to Endora School.
   4 Right—You're definitely bitch material. Keep working on it back at Evil Twin School.
   5 Right—Yup. You're a bitch alright. You've graduated to Joan Collins School.

How to Almost Catch the ROAD RUNNER

Since 1966, Wile E. Coyote (*evereadii-eatibus*) has been inches away from catching the *Road Runner* (*diqoutius-hot-rodis*) His lessons for us have been too numerous to count. We know, by heart, how to almost entrap the *Road Runner*. While reading over Wile E.'s methods, you should keep in mind whether you want to end up:

- ☐ Falling off a cliff
- ☐ Falling off a cliff and having something land on you
- ☐ Falling off a cliff, having something land on you, only to spring back up and get another piece of the cliff land on you
- ☐ Exploded
- ☐ Exploded and falling off a cliff
- ☐ Exploded and hit by a truck or train
- ☐ Flattened by a rock
- ☐ Launched off into orbit

Any one of the following methods may be used alone or combined with another to get the desired outcome. Use only the finest ACME products.

- ☐ Plant an ACME TNT telephone booth.
- ☐ Throw an ACME grenade so it hits a cactus and bounces back.
- ☐ Swing an ACME trapeze into a tunnel and hit the top.
- ☐ Use yourself as an arrow and fire yourself from an ACME bow into anything.
- ☐ Skateboard with a sail and ACME fan into or off of a tunnel or cliff.
- ☐ Fire an ACME Slingshot of dynamite that leaves the dynamite with you.
- ☐ Ride a giant ACME rocket toward a target and hit something to stop yourself, or fly to the stars.
- ☐ Slather your feet with ACME grease. Speed can be fun if you give up control.
- ☐ Position an ACME cannon on a cliff. The cliff breaks from the weight of the cannon, the cannon and you fall, the cannon aims at you, covers you, lands, fires, the cannon launches back up to the cliff, lands, breaks the cliff, the cannon and cliff fall on you.

Achievement

"I'm a pepper."
Dr. Pepper commercial

"I love it when a plan comes together."
Hannibal, *The A-Team*

"I am running with scissors."
Frasier, *Cheers*

Handy Pocket Guide #1

How to Tell the Difference Between SPEED BUGGY and SPEED RACER

In 1967 a Japanese-produced animation series *Speed Racer* struck the TV audience. In 1973, a Hanna-Barbera animated series took their television audience by storm with *Speed Buggy*. Today *Speed Racer* has grown into a cult classic, while the *Speed Buggy* series has fallen by the wayside. Here is an in-depth comparison of the two shows. Why would one stand the test of time and not the other? Draw your own conclusions.

Speed Buggy talks.	Speed Racer is a guy—he talks.
Speed Buggy and Tinker are chicken.	Speed Racer is a *guy.*
Speed Buggy is a car.	Speed Racer is a *guy.*
Speed Buggy has headlights for eyes.	Speed Racer has eyes for eyes.
Speed Buggy can go straight up a cliff.	Speed Racer needs a rope.
Speed Buggy coughs when he gets excited.	Speed Racer does other things.
Speed Buggy is nicknamed "Speedy."	Speed Racer is nicknamed "Speed Racer."
Speed Buggy likes to help people.	Speed Racer likes to drive fast.
Speed Buggy travels all over the U.S.	Speed Racer races cars.
Speed Buggy is a car.	Speed Racer is a *guy.*

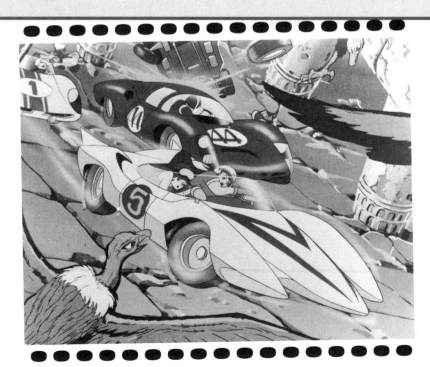

Handy Pocket Guide #2

How to Tell the Difference Between Donnie and Marie

Donnie and Marie Osmond were two of the nine extremely talented, extremely Mormon, Osmond children. Donnie had performed with his brothers in the Osmonds—a popular 70s bubblegum rock group who were sort of like the Jackson Five on Wonder Bread. Marie had country music in her blood. Together, they hosted *The Donnie and Marie Show*, one of the most popular variety shows of the late 70s.

For younger generations, and for those who just forgot, here's a handy pocket guide to telling Donnie and Marie apart.

MARIE

Feathered brown hair, long.

A little bit country.

Wore puffy shirts.

Good ice skater.

Sang, "May tomorrow be a perfect day."

Has a new sitcom.

DONNIE

Feathered brown hair, short.

A little bit rock-n-roll.

Wore purple socks.

Good tooth.

Sang, "May you find love and laughter along the way."

Has a new shirt.

Handy Pocket Guide #3

How to Tell the Difference Between Heather THE FALL GUY Thomas and Heather T.J. HOOKER—MELROSE PLACE Locklear

From 1982 to 1985, something very confusing was happening on ABC. On *The Fall Guy*, in which Lee Majors starred as a stunt man, there appeared a beautiful, blonde, capable, and intelligent woman named Heather. On a show called *T.J. Hooker*, in which William Shatner starred as a cop, there appeared a beautiful, blonde, capable, and intelligent woman named Heather.

One was Thomas; one was Locklear. One would vanish into anonymity; the other would become the star of one of the hottest prime-time soaps—*Melrose Place*.

Here is a handy pocket guide to telling these two women apart. Keep it close to your heart..

HEATHER THOMAS	HEATHER LOCKLEAR
Star of *The Fall Guy*.	Star of *T.J. Hooker*.
Once played a hooker.	Falls for the wrong guy.
Does her own stunts.	Does her own hair.
Signature line: "Colt, look out!"	Signature line: "Hooker, look out!"
Show created by Glen A. Larson, 80s power broker.	Now on *Melrose Place*, created by Aaron Spelling, 80s power broker.
Worked with loser actor Douglas Barr.	Worked with loser actor Adrian Zmed.

How to Change into HONG KONG PHOOEY

Changing from a mild-mannered janitor into *Hong Kong Phooey* (1974–1981)—number one superguy—wasn't easy. The switch from secret identity to superhero process was much more complex than on any other superhero show.

We've shown you how to do this here, but before you start the transformation, here are a few tips:

It is wise to assume either the identity of Penrod Pooch or Scatman Crothers before attempting to become *Hong Kong Phooey*.

Keep your arms and legs in at all times and have fun!

1. Ride the vacuum cleaner to the candy machine in the next room.

Note: *Keep the electric cord up and out of the way.*

2. Pass through the secret candy machine door. Be certain to hit the remote opener before reaching the candy machine. Remember, you will be riding on a vacuum cleaner that can reach speeds of up to four miles an hour.

3. Hop into the bottom drawer of an old file cabinet. Be sure that your leap into the cabinet is rough enough to wake your cat (who should be sleeping on top), as his assistance will be required in Step 6.

4. Even if your file drawers open easily, find a way to get stuck climbing to the top drawer and then say something like, "Darn this file cabinet" while climbing down to the middle drawer. Remember, you are still inside the file cabinet, so the effect will have a heightened echo.

5. When you leap from the cabinet in your *Hong Kong Phooey* robe and eye mask, kung fu the air and say one of the following:

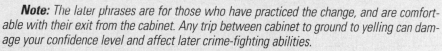

    a. "Ya ah, ya ha!"

    b. "Yo-si-ya!"

    c. "Ha-soo-ya!"

    d. "Pho-ya!"

    e. "Zo-ti-zto-ka-ya!"

    f. "Do-shtane-zo-kaye-ha!"

Note: *The later phrases are for those who have practiced the change, and are comfortable with their exit from the cabinet. Any trip between cabinet to ground to yelling can damage your confidence level and affect later crime-fighting abilities.*

6. Have your cat open the ironing board from the wall.

7. Spring up so the ironing board closes and launches you into the air vent.

8. Sail down the air vent and when you emerge from the bottom, bounce off an old couch, out the window, and into the dumpster.

Note: *This requires pre-placement of tools. Specifically, the couch and the dumpster. It may also be wise to make sure the window is open.*

9. Open the side of the dumpster and drive off in the Phooey Mobile. If need be, karate chop the Phooey gong (in the glovebox) and change the Phooey Mobile into the Phooey Chopper.

You should now be in full *Hong Kong Phooey* attire and in transit to the site of a crime. If not, read back over these instructions and start again from any step you may have overlooked. Good luck. And don't forget to give some credit to Sergeant Flint.

"You can have the banana and whatever's inside, or you can choose what's behind door number 3."
Monty Hall, *Let's Make a Deal*

"You know, medicine is not an exact science, but we are learning all the time. Why, just fifty years ago they thought a disease like your daughter's was caused by demonic possession or witchcraft. But nowadays, we know ᵗʰat Isabelle is suffering from an imbalance of bodily humors, perhaps caused by a toad or a small dwarf living in her stomach."
Theodoric of York, *Saturday Night Live*

"Sir, you are a superb starship captain. But as a taxi driver, you leave much to be desired."
Spock, *Star Trek*

I'm the sole survivor.
Stay Alive commercial

"I'm going to the back seat of my car and I won't be back for ten minutes!"
Homer Simpson, *The Simpsons*

"I once whooped me five lumberjacks!"
Uncle Jack, *Grizzly Adams*

"At First Citywide Change Bank, we just make change. A lot of people don't realize that change is a two-way street. You can come in with sixteen quarters, eight dimes, and four nickels—we can give you a five-dollar bill. Or, we can give you five singles. Or two singles, eight quarters, and ten dimes. You'd be amazed at the variety of options you have."
Bank Commercial, *Saturday Night Live*

There is no other pair of Czechoslovakian brothers who cruise and swing so successfully in tight slacks.
The Festrunk Brothers, *Saturday Night Live*

The Malachi Crunch

The Malachi Crunch is a dangerous method of rendering opponents' cars useless. It requires two people driving in two cars on either side of a victim. When the victim is at a standstill, the Malachi attackers back into either side of said car. This move crunches the victim between the two Malachi cars, hence the term "Malachi Crunch."

The Malachi Crunch, to date, has only been avoided through one method.

How to Escape the Malachi Crunch
Like Pinky and Fonzie

Rocko and Count Malachi destroyed twenty-seven cars with the famous Malachi Crunch. And only one-half of the cars were actually demolished in the demolition derby.

It took the love and coolness of Fonzie and Pinky to break the Malachis. They came onto *Happy Days* near the end of its ten-year run (1974–1984), and with the help of the entire *Happy Days* gang, Mr. and Mrs. C, Richie, Potsie, Ralph Malph, Joanie, and the Pinkettes, Fonzie and Pinky narrowly escaped and defeated the dreaded Malachis and avoided the Crunch.

They humiliated the Malachi brothers.

Should you ever run into them, here are the never-before-revealed secrets to Fonzie and Pinky's great escape. Use them wisely.

The Fonzie and Pinky Escape

Know that your opponents are honorless weasles. So come prepared. You will need two walkie-talkies, a blow dryer, and all of your cool.

When the derby is underway, use your walkie-talkies. Tell your partner, constantly, to watch her nose, watch her nose. This will make the Malachis think you are on the defensive. Be ready at the blow dryer. The Malachi method has been known to use the blowing-flour-in-the-opponents-eyes trick. So be at the ready. When the flour comes your way, turn on the blow dryer and reverse its effects. One Malachi car will be temporarily out of commision, but do not take this opportunity. Let them think you are scared. Stop your car in the middle of the derby ground and let the Malachis get into position. Then, stall your car.

The Malachis will now think three things: You are on the defensive; you are scared; and you are helpless. They will let down all of their defenses thinking all they have left is to crunch you. Let the moment be. They will rev their engines, bounce their front axles off the ground, call you on the walkie-talkie and tell you goodbye.

Now for the escape. Tell them goodbye and let them start to reverse into you. Once they are underway, simply hit the dashboard of your car so that it starts, and back up out of their path. The Malachi brothers' cars will hit each other and you will have escaped the inescapable Malachi Crunch.

12

A BRADY NEVER GOES BACK ON HER PROMISE: TRUTH, JUSTICE, AND THE TELEVISION WAY

t is our beliefs that shape us. Our opinions and perspectives determine how we deal with any given situation. Without beliefs we would not know whether to turn left or right, love or hate, get house blend or espresso. We need our beliefs.

Our beliefs come first from our families. Then our friends. Then our experiences. Then from TV. We had the Bradys to teach us about family values; we had Frank Burns to teach us about towing the line and trusting superiors; we had Quincy to teach us to look beyond the facts and trust our gut instincts; we had Cookie Monster to teach us about priorities (cookies first, then the world).

● ● ● ● ● ● ● ● ● ● ● ● ● ● ● ● ● ●

"Unless we each conform, unless we obey orders, unless we follow our leaders blindly, there is no possible way we can remain free."
Frank Burns, *M*A*S*H*

"Dear advertisers: I am disgusted with the way old people are depicted on television. We are not all vibrant, fun-loving sex maniacs. Some of us are bitter, resentful individuals who remember the good old days when entertainment was bland and inoffensive."
Grandpa Simpson, *The Simpsons*

"Uh, oh. Smell like the law, don't it?"
Voice Over, *The Dukes of Hazzard*

MICHAEL STEADMAN: You wanna know if I accept that a star led three wise men to a manger with a lady who claims she hadn't had sex, just had a baby who was the son of God?
HOPE STEADMAN: And I'm supposed to accept that a tiny drop of oil lasted eight days, and that six men with bows and arrows defeated the entire Roman Legion?
ThirtySomething

"Everything is a moral issue with you! If the dry cleaner over-charges you it's the breakdown of modern civilization. If you're nailed for speeding then suddenly we're living in a police state."
Michael Steadman, *ThirtySomething*

"Chocolate cookie very important. Mean a lot to me . . . oh and this butter cookie, me not want to make butter cookie feel bad. Butter cookie very important. Mean a lot to me. In fact all cookie mean a lot to me . . . KAWABUNGA!"
Cookie Monster, *Sesame Street*

"When I was drafted I had a clear understanding with the Pentagon: no guns. I'll carry your books, I'll carry a torch, I'll carry a tune, I'll carry on, carry over, carry forward, Cary Grant, cash and carry, 'Carry Me Back to Old Virginia,' I'll even 'hari-kari' if you show me how, but I will not carry a gun!"
Hawkeye Pierce, *M*A*S*H*

"I don't want to see a guilty man go free any more than you want an innocent man to go to jail."
Quincy, *Quincy*

DAISY DUKE: How'd you get to be so wise?
UNCLE JESSE: What're old men for?
The Dukes of Hazzard

SHIRLEY: The only parties we've been to are bring-your-own.
LAVERNE: I like bringing my own. That way I know what I'm gettin'.
Laverne and Shirley

Do You React As Well As Quincy Does When Things "Just Don't Add Up?"

A Personality Test

There are those who persist in proving what they see as the truth—whose guts tell them the answers. These folks follow their beliefs and continue the search no matter what the evidence says. They look at the circumstances from every angle.

No one did this better on TV than *Quincy*. From 1976–1983 *The Odd Couple*'s Jack Klugman cleaned up his act and started cutting up dead bodies. With his trusty sidekick Sam Fujiyama, Quincy looked beyond the facts and chased the truth.

Here is a test to see how persistent you are in your own quest. Here's a hint—trust your hunches.

1. When someone shows you a picture of a friend and claims he killed someone, you:
    a) Say, "Get out of here, you loony bat."
    b) Say, "As much as I don't want to believe it, let's go to work to prove it."
    c) Silently frown, wrinkle your forehead, and look quickly, fearfully, at Sam.
2. When you spot a cut on the hand of a suspected murderer, you:
    a) Get them a band-aid and some ointment.
    b) Ask them where it came from.
    c) Ask them where it came from, frown, wrinkle your forehead, and carry on as if you know they're lying about something.
3. When the electrophoresis results don't prove your theory about who killed whom, you:
    a) Blow it off, close the case, and go get a taco.
    b) Double-check the samples to be absolutely certain.
    c) Frown, wrinkle your forehead, and stare at the results wondering if there is some way to fake your blood type.
4. When you talk to the doctor of a murder suspect and he tells you that his patient's medical history and present condition don't match, you:
    a) Say, "Well, that's tough. I guess science needs some more work. Hey, Doc, you wanna go get a beer?"
    b) Say, "Hmm. If he's not who he was, and shouldn't be who he is, I wonder who he's going to become."
    c) Frown, wrinkle your forehead, and say "I've gotta follow this hunch."
5. When you have finally proved what you thought all along, you:
    a) Strut around the room like a peacock and say,"I was right, I was right!"
    b) Sit down in a chair and cry, "Why! Why do people kill each other! What's wrong with a little peace!"
    c) Smile, wrinkle your forehead, throw the test results down, and humbly walk away thinking, "I knew it all along."

Answer Key: "C" is always correct.
Scoring:
    1 Right—You're no Quincy. Go back to grade school and dissect worms.
    2 Right—You're no Quincy, but keep at it.
    3 Right—You're no Quincy, but you might be able to pass for Sam.
    4 Right—You're no Quincy, but you might pass for Oscar.
    5 Right—You're Quincy alright. Nice work, Quince.

PINKY TUSCADERO: You're wrong, though.
FONZIE: I am not wrrrrrooooo . . .
Happy Days

"I never go anywhere that I can't say 'full house' in the native tongue."
Max, *Hart to Hart*

"I've made up my mind. I'm going to be Jewish . . . I want a Bar Mitzvah. You walk in a boy, and come out a man. And that's for me. Shalom!"
Arnold Drummond, *Diff'rent Strokes*

"A Brady never goes back on her promise."
Mike Brady, *The Brady Bunch*

" . . . but know this: You can cut me off from the civilized world. You can incarcerate me with two moronic cellmates. You can torture me with your thrice-daily swill. But you cannot break the spirit of a Winchester. My voice shall be heard from this wilderness, and I shall be delivered from this fetid and festering sewer."
Charles Emerson Winchester III, *M*A*S*H*

"Those little lines around your mouth, those crow's-feet around your eyes, the millimeter your derriere has slipped in the last decade—they're all just nature's way of telling you you've got nine holes left to play, so get out there and have a good time."
David Addison, *Moonlighting*

"It's no crime to act your age."
Bill Gannon, *Dragnet*

"If you plant rice, rice will grow. If you plant fear, fear will grow."
Caine, *Kung Fu*

"If there's anything that can make me nervous, it's an angry genie."
Roger, *I Dream of Jeannie*

"Fear is the only darkness."
Master Po, *Kung Fu*

"Life is a corridor and death merely a door."
Caine, *Kung Fu*

"You know I hate funerals. If it were up to me I wouldn't even go to my own."
George Jefferson, *The Jeffersons*

"I hate moral dilemmas."
Jake, *Melrose Place*

"I might as well be dead. . . . Well, I'm going to bed, son. Good-night. If I'm lucky I'll sleep until angel Gabriel wakes me up. . . . If not, I'll see you at the usual time."
Fred Sanford, *Sanford and Son*

BIG BIRD: So where's Mr. Hooper? I wanna give him this picture.
BOB: Well, Big Bird . . . Mr Hooper died.
BIG BIRD: Oh, okay. Well, I'll give it to him when he comes back.
Sesame Street

KIT: It must be very difficult to erase people from one's memory bank.
MICHAEL KNIGHT: That's the problem, Kit. You don't. You can't.
KIT: If that's true, then they become a permanent part of you.
MICHAEL: The best of 'em do, buddy . . . the best of 'em do just that.
Knight Rider

YOU WOULDN'T LIKE ME WHEN I'M MAD: INSULTS AND TOUGH GUY TALK

T ough talk and insults have always been part of our culture. From Ulysses to Jason of the Argonauts, Sir Galahad to Baretta, Joe Friday to Daffy Duck, we have learned to stand up to the bullies of the world by following the examples they set.

All tough guys have one thing in common—they are cool under pressure and quick witted. They are all willing to go the distance—to do whatever it takes to win their battles. Here's courage at its best, according to the Gospels of the Antennae.

● ● ● ● ● ● ● ● ● ● ● ● ● ● ● ● ● ●

"Drip-a-long Daffy's the name. Anyone care to shoot it out? Man to man! Under western skies! West o' the Pecos! Tumbleweeds at ten paces! Ten thousand heads a cow! Cut 'em off at the pass?! Lariats?! . . . Anyone for tennis? Anyone . . ."
Drip-a-long Daffy, *Looney Tunes*

BAD GUY: Tell me Mr. West, have you ever heard of the word *Varkalik?*
JAMES WEST: What does it mean? Stand off?
BAD GUY: Not quite. It is almost untranslatable. But in this case it means you are alone, unguarded, and you may expect a blow to the head—now!
The Wild, Wild West

"Move, and I'll slit you like a hog."
Tony Baretta, *Baretta*

"If I had time to clean up the mess, I'd shoot you."
J.R. Ewing, *Dallas*

YOSEMITE SAM: Be you the mean hombre that's a-hankerin' for a heap a trouble, stranger? . . . Well, be ya?!
BUGS BUNNY: I be.
Bugs Bunny

"I warn you, I've got claws."
Erica Kane, *All My Children*

"Come on, let's go. Only if we catch you here again . . . gonna make chop suey out of you!"
Bad Guy to Caine, *Kung Fu*

"A vulture has instinct—what's your excuse?"
Lieutenant, *Simon and Simon*

"It's a shame you don't live in India . . . You'd be sacred there."
Mr. Roper, *Three's Company*

TODD: Uuuhhh . . . Lisa, your pancakes are ready.
LISA LUPNER: Todd, that's so funny I forgot to laugh.
Saturday Night Live

"I shall get him when he returns. He's got to cross my mountain when he returns. And then, no more being the nice guy."
Winter Warlock, *Santa Claus Is Coming to Town*

ELLEN: You're an incredibly nice person, Michael.
MICHAEL: Nice? Nice. Kiss-a-death, babe.
ThirtySomething

How to Run the Good Guys Off the Road, According to the Bad Guys

For years we watched the battles of good against evil. Mostly good was victorious (at least, by the end of the hour). But the bad guys had to reign for a while in order to make for a good hour of drama and chasing around.

Here's the formula that was used by the bad guys from shows throughout TV history, from *The Greatest American Hero* to *Simon and Simon*, from *T.J. Hooker* to *Wonder Woman*.

1. Get a Buick.

2. Buy a bad suit. It doesn't matter where you're going—always look completely out of place. If you're downtown and they wear grey, wear blue.

3. On your first meeting with the good guys, be dumb but forceful. For example, yell to them that you're coming to get them when you're a good fifty feet away—that way they have time to start running.

4. Give the good guys a head start. Looking at your partner or pausing to try to figure out what the good guys are doing is a good way to stall and give them a few extra seconds. Always let them get in their car and start driving before you even start your Buick.

5. Start the chase.

Note: *It's not necessary to peel out or kick up dust, but if you don't want to hit the guy on the bike who's about to cross in front of you, it helps to give him fair warning that something's going down.*

6. Don't get too close too soon. And turn wide around a couple of bends so they know you mean business.

7. Come right up on their tails. Drop back a few feet and then bump them. (For heightened effect, lurch forward as the car hits.) If two or three hits doesn't send them to the shoulder, proceed to the next step.

8. Pull up parallel to their car and give them a good grimace. After a few moments, swerve left and then right, scraping the side of their car. If you're approaching a turn, this side swipe coupled with a hard turn should do the trick and knock them off the road.

9. Congratulations! You have just pushed the good guys off the road. Depending upon how much time is left in the show, you either let them get away or put them in the back of your car. Either way, be sure to brush off your pants and look off into the distance at the end.

How to Jump in a Car
Like THE DUKES OF HAZZARD

From 1979–1985 driver's education teaching was set back about fifty years—for it was in these years that *The Dukes of Hazzard* raced across dirt roads and television screens. It was because of this show that millions of young teenagers injured themselves getting in their cars. Read on, and you'll get the picture.

1. Turn on the engine of, preferably, a bright orange Dodge with a confederate flag painted on the roof.
2. Play a Waylon Jennings tape.
3. Roll down the window. (Hint: This is the most important step. The Dukes actually had no windows in the General Lee.)
4. Hitch up your just-tight-enough Wrangler jeans.
5. Back up about twenty feet on the side of the car with the open window.
6. Have a friend yell, "It's the Dukes! Get 'em, Cletus!"
7. Run toward the window and jump in, feet first.
8. You're either in the car or in a whole lot of pain.
9. Floor the gas pedal and head for home, where Daisy May and Uncle Jesse will be waitin'.

"It's just that when you see a grown guy in a sailor suit chasing a big buxom blonde down a passageway, the word *doctor* doesn't come to mind."
Gopher, *The Love Boat*

FLORENCE: Is there something you don't like about my cooking?
GEORGE: Yeah—eating it.
The Jeffersons

"You girls can't eat here. You're waitresses, not people."
Mel Sharpels, *Alice*

How to Catch a Crook, According to SCOOBY DOO

Scooby and the gang from the Mystery Van—Fred, Velma, and Daphne—have years of crime fighting and paranormal debunking experience (the show ran off and on, on CBS and then ABC, from 1969–1986). So why was it that they always solved the mystery in the same accidental way? Velma lost her glasses; Fred and Daphne set up a trap after going off alone (what was that about?); or Scoob and Shaggy bumbled into it. No matter—they got the job done. Here's how you can do the same.

1. After searching fruitlessly through the first half of the episode, listen as Fred finally maps out the plan.
2. Scooby and Shaggy will act as bait—only after being bribed by a Scooby Snack—and will lure the mysterious phantoms into the room.
3. Scooby and Shaggy will stop in the middle of the room, underneath a large net that the gang just happens to have.
4. Scooby and Shaggy will jump away, the net will drop, and they'll have the phantoms!

What actually happens is different. Scooby and Shaggy do in fact run into the phantoms, usually accidentally, with Shaggy feeling around in the dark and finding a pair of evil looking eyes that clearly aren't Scooby's.

1. Shaggy, realizing that this isn't Scoob, gives a large "Gulp!" and says, with all his might, "Scooooooooob! Let's get outtaheeeeeeeeeere!"
2. Scooby and Shaggy run as fast as they can, spinning their legs underneath them.
3. They run into the room with the trap, and Shaggy drops his flashlight.
4. When the phantoms come in after them and Scooby and Shaggy try to jump away, Shaggy gets his pant leg or shirt caught on a loose nail, and cannot jump. He and Scooby become caught in the net as it drops. The phantoms are still loose.
5. As the phantoms run closer to their now-trapped prey, one of them trips over Shaggy's flashlight, and they all run into each other, slamming into the wall and knocking each other out.
6. The trap has worked! Once again the gang has solved the mystery, and once again it was Mr. Whithers (weren't they all named Whithers?), the old butler—night watchman—deliveryman—disgruntled employee!
7. Treat yourself to another Scooby Snack and say, "Roobyroobyroo!"

The Anaconda Narration from
MUTUAL OF OMAHA'S WILD KINGDOM

Mutual of Omaha's Wild Kingdom was perhaps the most prominent and influential animal documentary. From 1963 to 1971 it fed our interest in the animal world, and was thus the precursor to today's Discovery Channel. Further, and more importantly, with the overlapping broadcast of *Star Trek* (1966–1969) a marked similarity may be seen between William Shatner's trademark of pausing after every third word and Marlin Perkins's enunciation of every last syllable while narrating his animal adventures. Makes you wonder . . .

The Anaconda Episode

Stan decided to lasso the anaconda and drag him to shore . . . got 'im!

The anaconda coiled immediately, reacting to the lasso. The anaconda has tremendous strength and can literally squeeze the breath and life out of his victims. When you take on a twenty-foot anaconda, you wanna be ready for anything.

What I wasn't ready for was the deep hole in the middle of the pond. And all of a sudden, I was in over my head. Then the anaconda had the advantage, because my leverage was gone, and I was fighting the huge reptile in its preferred element . . . water.

With a snake around your neck, the greatest danger is from suffocation. He kept pulling us into deep water. The anaconda exerted great pressure and its weight kept me off balance. We worked the anaconda away from the deep water and it became easier to find solid footing on the bottom.

The solid footing gave me some leverage. With leverage again, it became possible to control the head of the anaconda, while Stan began stuffing its tail into the capture bag. It was not long before Stan and I had the huge anaconda in the bag, so to speak, and ready for its trip to a zoo in Europe.

"Blistering barnacles, Professor. You're unbearable."
Captain, *Tintin*

"Grandpa, you are the world's oldest goofball."
Herman Munster, *The Munsters*

"You know, there's something to be said for what you think . . . and that something is 'garbage!'"
George Jefferson, *The Jeffersons*

"If there's anything I can't stand it's a company Octopussaurus."
Fred Flintstone, *The Flintstones*

MRS. GARRETT: Jo is terrific. She makes sure we don't under-sell or overbuy. She's a real watchdog.·
BLAIRE: For Christmas I think I'll get her a flea collar.
   The Facts of Life

"Sarge, if I thought there was gonna be any fighting, I never would have joined the army."
   Corporal Agarn, *F-Troop*

BATMAN: Anytime you're ready, Clock King.
CLOCK KING: Just give me a minute . . . a minute to activate my counter-attack activator!
   Batman

"The only good human is a dead human."
   General Urko, *The Planet of the Apes*

"Look, Benson, don't make us lean on ya', 'cause when my partner leans he goes in hot and heavy and deep enough to strike oil! Now either you talk to us here . . . or we go downtown and talk all night."
   Bill Gannon, *Dragnet*

"Clayton, do you ever have an unexpressed thought?"
   Benson Dubois, *Benson*

"Jan is not a creep. She's a super creep!"
   Peter Brady, *The Brady Bunch*

"Jane you ignorant slut!"
   Dan Ackroyd, *"Point Counterpoint," Saturday Night Live*

SUE ELLEN: Which slut are you sleeping with tonight?
J.R.: Does it matter? Whoever she is she'll be more interesting than the slut I'm looking at right now.
   Dallas

"Please, Mr. Wolf—don't steal my sheep."
   Droopy, *Droopy*

How to Win a Fight Like Captain Kirk

"The bad guy would be coming at me, and I'd run up, jump in the air, and fling toward him with my feet. It was really just like the flying drop kicks pro wrestlers use. I loved that move. I used it all the time and of course every time I used it within a *Star Trek* episode, the bad guy would just sort of flop over unconscious any time I even came close to kicking him. Over the years I'd gotten pretty used to doing this, and I have to admit, I really thought this was cool, this was Kirk's move."

William Shatner, *Star Trek Memories*

Captain Kirk was our hero—handsome, smug, and tough, even though we all knew he was losing his hair. Throughout *Star Trek's* five-year mission (which ran only three in prime time), he fought, loved, and smirked his way to fame. But mostly fought. In virtually every episode, after the guy in the red shirt died, Kirk would be forced into hand-to-hand combat with some-

one—human, Klingon, Romulan, whatever. Kirk didn't care. He'd kiss or hit anything. And he'd do it well.

Here's a guide to Kirk's technique. Read it, and don't ever let anyone sucker punch you.

1. Distract the person you're about to hit. If he's a Klingon or alien, confuse him by making something up, insult his wife, his ship, or his honor.
2. Turn around as if you're walking away from the situation—then sucker punch him.
3. Take down as many of them as you can while Spock pinches the necks of anyone within his reach. Wonder why, if Spock had superhuman strength, did he spend all his time pinching people?
4. When one of your opponents holds you by the torso, swing your legs up, kick the opponent charging you, and land on the opponent who's holding you. This is called the "Kirk Kick."

Note: *Never confuse this move with "Kick Kirk."*

5. At some point in the fight, you must rip your shirt, exposing your nipple. At the end of the fight, the corner of your lip must always be bleeding, even if no one came near it.
6. Don't trust an opponent who is still conscious—always knock him out with a small table or a rock.
7. Breathe heavily at the end of the fight, wipe the corner of your lip, say something witty, and contact the *Enterprise* to be beamed aboard.

How to Win the "Rabbit Season!—Duck Season!" Argument, According to Bugs Bunny

The "Rabbit Season!—Duck Season!" argument has entered the annals of cartoon lore as one of the classic *Looney Tunes* exchanges between the wascally wabbit Bugs Bunny and the dethpicable Daffy Duck. It's inescapable illogic, rapid-fire pace, and "Who's on First?" mentality have made it a cherished exchange for all Saturday morning TV viewers. Moreover, the lesson it teaches is an essential one—listen carefully.

1. When Elmer Fudd walks up with his gun, look at Daffy, as if you're afraid.
2. Daffy will tell Elmer to shoot you. Point to a sign on a tree reading "Rabbit Season," and insist that it's "rabbit theathon!"
3. When Elmer points his rifle at Bugs, tear down the "Rabbit Season" sign to reveal a "Duck Season" sign, and calmly inform him that it's duck season!
4. Daffy will tear down the "Duck Season" sign and point out to Elmer, who is now pointing his rifle at him, that it isn't duck season, but rather as the new sign reveals, "It's rabbit theathon!"
5. Now is the key part of the exchange. The dialogue should run as follows: with each line accompanied by the tearing down of another sign:

BUGS: Duck season!
DAFFY: Rabbit theathon!
BUGS: Duck season!
DAFFY: Rabbit theathon!
BUGS: Duck season!
DAFFY: Rabbit theathon!
Bugs (*pretending to tear down the next-to-last sign*): Rabbit season!
DAFFY: Duck theathon!
ELMER: BOOOM!

The rifle explodes in Daffy's face, shooting his beak to the back of his head.
6. Bugs chomps on a carrot, satisfied, as Daffy pulls his beak to the front of his face and says, "You're dethpicable."

"I don't know why I did it, I don't know why I enjoyed it, and I don't know why I'll do it again."

Bart Simpson, *The Simpsons*

"You thieves think I'm a regular passenger. Well, I'm not! In reality I'm Quick Draw McGraw. Does that strike a note of terror in your das-tard-ly hearts?"

Quick Draw McGraw, *Quick Draw Mcgraw*

MR. T: Gimme a cup of coffee!
WAITER: How do you want it?
MR. T: In a cup, fool!

The A-Team

"Now, if anyone tries to tell me he doesn't like Mr. and Mrs. T's Bloody Mary Mix, I say to him, 'Shut up old man! Shut up!' And then I kill him to death. I kill the man who doesn't drink it. But I pity him first. It's a bloody shame. It's Mr. and Mrs. T's Bloody Mary Mix. Buy it, or I'll kill you."

Mr. T, *Saturday Night Live*

ELMER FUDD: Thewe's something scwewy awound hewe.
BUGS BUNNY: Eeeh . . . could be you, doc.

Bugs Bunny

I WOULDA WORN MY TUXEDO, BUT MY POLO PONY ATE IT: NONSEQUITURS AND MEANINGLESS WISDOM

F rom confusion, some say, we learn the most. For that is when our minds are the most open to knowledge—when all predispositions and prejudices are tossed out because the world we know is upside down.

Our TV friends got laughs out of us through nonsequiturs and meaningless nonsense, but they also got us to think. In this chapter, you'll find those humorous TV moments that threw you for a loop, from the meaningless sarcasm of Squiggy to the redundant simple-mindedness of *Speed Buggy;* from the poignant nonsense of Hawkeye Pierce to the witticisms of Mork from Ork.

Find meaning where you will.

● ● ● ● ● ● ● ● ● ● ● ● ● ● ● ● ●

"Skipper wanted me to be Skipper in case anything happened to Skipper."
Gilligan, *Gilligan's Island*

"Okay, we've got another deal coming up and I need a pumpkin for this one."
Monty Hall, *Let's Make a Deal*

"Ah! The old drug-his-prunes, fake-the-fight, ransack-the-apartment, and switch-places-with-the-admiral trick."
Maxwell Smart, *Get Smart*

"This breakfast is good enough to eat!"
Chrissy, *Three's Company*

"I've eaten a river of liver and an ocean of fish! I've eaten so much fish, I'm ready to grow gills! I've eaten so much liver, I can only make love if I'm smothered in bacon and onions!"
Hawkeye Pierce, *M*A*S*H*

"Will ya' George? Huh? Huh? Will ya'? Huh George? Huh? . . . George? Where did you go at, George?"
Benny the Cat, *Looney Tunes*

"Dinosaurs are extinct, so you never can tell where they're liable to show up."
Hadji, *Johnny Quest*

SAM: Where're you going?
QUINCY: I'm gonna find out how a man can go into a surgeon's office in apparent good health, and in a few hours be wheeled out in a coma.
Quincy

"Speedy thinking, Speedy."
Debbie, *Speed Buggy*

MICHAEL KNIGHT: Your buddies, are they racing tonight?
RACER: I doubt it. The heat's just too hot.
Knight Rider

Mutual of Omaha's Wild Kingdom is presented to you by Mutual of Omaha.
Mutual of Omaha's Wild Kingdom

"My days as a hairless wonder are over."
Gumby, *Gumby*

DATA: There's nothing out there; absolutely nothing.
GEORDI: Well it's a damn ugly nothing!
Star Trek: The Next Generation

Radar: How can I ever thank you?
HAWKEYE: Well, you can give us your firstborn.
B.J.: And an order of fries.
M*A*S*H

"I woulda worn my tuxedo but my polo pony ate it."
Squiggy, *Laverne and Shirley*

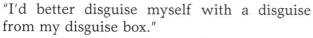

"I'd better disguise myself with a disguise from my disguise box."
Hong Kong Phooey, *Hong Kong Phooey*

"That weirdo's getting weirder."
George Jefferson, *The Jeffersons*

"Eddie, you naughty naughty boy! You traded your grandfather for a squirrel!"
Lily Munster, *The Munsters*

ROCKY: If they blow up the dam, think of what will happen to those poor people in Frostbite Falls!
BULLWINKLE: Those poor people will get mighty soggy!
Rocky and Bullwinkle

Knock knock.
Who's there?
Alec.
Alec who?
I like beer! It makes me jolly!
After hearin' a joke like that, I'm gonna need a whole six pack.
Hee Haw

How to Teach Your Friends the Difference Between "Near" and "Far," According to Grover

We have learned many things from *Sesame Street* over the years. We've learned how to count. We've learned that numbers and letters sponsor shows. We've learned that *agua* means "water," *abierto* means "open," and *cerrado* means "closed."

One of our most memorable teachers was lovable, furry old Grover. It was he who taught us one of life's most valuable lessons—the difference between *near* and *far*.

You can try this one at home.

1. Have your friends stand at the corner of one block.

2. Stand close to your friends and speak the following words, in a lovable, furry voice. "Hello everybody. Today we are going to learn the difference between *near* and *far*."

3. Take a step closer to your friends and say, "Now (your name) is near."

4. As fast as you can, run to the far corner of the block and yell, "Can you see me now? Now (your name) is far!"

5. As fast as you can, run back to your friends' corner. "See the difference? I am now near, but I was far! Let's try it again."

6. Step close to your friends again. "Now, (your name) is near."

7. As fast as you can, run to the far corner of the block and yell, "And now (your name) is far!"

8. As fast as you can, clip-clopping the whole way, run back to your friends' corner. Say, "Near!"

9. As fast as you can, clip-clopping the whole way, run back to the far corner of the block and yell, "Far!"

10. As fast as you can, run back to your friends. Say, "See the difference?"

11. Now wait, and see their reaction. If they don't immediately leave, completely disgusted, repeat the entire exercise until you drive them away.

The Vitameatavegemin Speech
from I LOVE LUCY

Here's one of Lucy's best moments—her first and only stint as a TV commercial star—the Vitameatavegemin girl. Lucy has been hired to promote Vitameatavegemin, a Geritol-like health aid that happens to have a lot of alcohol in it. Lucy does the first take beautifully:

Hello friends. I'm your Vitameatavegemin girl. Are you tired, run down, and listless? Do you poop out at parties? Are you unpopular? The answer to all your problems is in this little bottle: Vitameatavegemin, containing vitamins, meal, vegetables, and minerals. Yes, with Vitameatavegemin you can spoon your way to health. All you do is take a spoonful after every meal. (*Take spoonful and swallow.*) It's so tasty, too! Just like candy! So why don't you join the thousands of happy, peppy people and get a great big bottle of Vitameatavegemin today. That's Vita-meata-vegemin.

All goes well—until Lucy has to repeat take after take, and she becomes heavily intoxicated by the end of the day and her spunky delivery has turned to a drunken slur:

Well, I'm your vita-veeda-vigee-vat girl. Are you tired, run down, listless? . . . Well, are you? Do you pop out at parties? Are you unpoopular? The answer to alllllllll your problems is in this li'l ole bottle—Vita-meeta-vegemin. . . . That's it!

Great Paul Lynde One-Liners
from THE HOLLYWOOD SQUARES

The Hollywood Squares ran from 1966 through 1989, hosted first by Peter Marshall and later by John Davidson. The show featured a panel of nine semi-celebrities, positioned in each of the nine spots on a vertical tic-tac-toe board. None got more laughs than the sardonic Paul Lynde.

PETER: Before a cow will give you any milk, she has to have something very important. What?
PAUL: An engagement ring.

PETER: According to *Movie Life* magazine, Ann-Margret would like to start having babies, soon, but her husband wants her to wait a while. Why?
PAUL: He's out of town.

PETER: Who stays pregnant for a longer period of time, your wife or your elephant?
PAUL: Who told you about my elephant?

PETER: According to psychologists, when a child begins to get curious about sex, what is the one question he will most ask his mommy and daddy?
PAUL: Where can I get some?

PETER: Do female frogs croak?
PAUL: If you hold their little heads under water.

How to Correctly Use Your Wonder Twin Powers, According to Zan and Jayna from THE SUPERFRIENDS

Zan and Jayna, the Wonder Twins, were a teenage pair of superheroes who, with their monkey, Gleek, assisted the Superfriends (1973–1985 on ABC) in fighting the Legion of Doom.

More often than not, Zan and Jayna's powers got them into trouble, but in a touch of weekly irony that appeared too frequently not to be noticed, it was often the Wonder Twins (or Gleek) who saved the day.

Here's how they did it, and how you can, too.

1. Find a friend and buy a pair of matching rings.
2. Put on purple tights.
3. See the looming danger approaching, perhaps Gleek innocently eating a banana while an escaped puma from the zoo, a result of the havoc caused by Lex Luthor's metal-decaying ray, is behind him.
4. Make fists with your ring hands, and say, in unison, "Wonder Twin Powers—activate!"
5. Touch rings.
6. Zan can assume the form of anything water-based. Here are some of the best options:
    An ice bucket
    An ice crowbar
    Water vapor
    An ice jail
    A puddle of water
7. Jayna can assume the form of anything animal. Here are some of her best choices:
    A gorilla
    A pelican
    A giant snake
    An ant
    A mouse
8. In the case of the escaped puma, Zan assumes the form of an ice cage. Jayna becomes a female puma.
9. Jayna lures the puma into the cage, runs out the door, and Zan slams himself shut.
10. Once again the Wonder Twins have saved the day. Gleek stands outside the cage, taunting the puma until the zookeepers come to take him away. Zan and Jayna touch fists again, and say, "Wonder Twin Powers—deactivate!"

The Ministry of Silly Walks, A Guide

There have been plenty of wacky British comedies, though none has been as popular as *Monty Python's Flying Circus* (1969–1974).

There is the Ministry of Defense, the Ministry of Agriculture, and for those of us not so concerned with politics, there is the Ministry of Silly Walks. Here's a guide.

THE MINISTRY OF SILLY WALKS, MONTY PYTHON,

DEPT. #574923048958-384-A

The Ministry, being the party of the first part, and its members, being the party of the party of the first part, is founded upon the following principles, which, by all members and associates is approved and protected by law and all of its legal preceding precedents relating to and evolving from. It has been and shall continue to be established that:

1. The Ministry of Silly Walks is a Ministry.
2. All and every department within said Ministry shall be protected and enhanced by the ways and means of Ministerial ways and means.
3. Members and associates to determine the need and/or present desire for, therefore, creation of and adherence to instances involving a single, or some plural Silly Walks.
4. Therefore and to it, the following definitions shall suffice for proof thereof as to definitions of terms:

   a. Ministry—Any organization duly supported by government and therefore both establishment and members supported by said government.

   b. Of, The—Simple articles surrounding other nouns, try not to think too hard about them.

   c. Silly—Anything that is not serious, and therefore relates to the scale of Humors, being from Funny to Comical to Hysterical, that to be said Silly falls within its own lines of Funny-Comedy though not Comical-Funny, and perhaps though leading to Hysterical-Silly-Funny-Comedy.

   d. Walks—A walk or walks depends upon moving forward or backward or side to side or up or down, or in some various direction, and thus taking one's body in that direction, though not necessarily in that order.

Practice:

A silly walk may entail in theory moving the body, at least the feet, in one direction, though not necessarily in the same direction as the body.

Steps:

1. Stand erect. Hands at sides. Feet together.
2. Slouch at the back. Knees bent. Leg extended directly forward.
3. One foot on ground on tiptoe. Other leg brought right up to eye level.
4. Step forward. Back straight. Rear leg extends full step.
5. Rear leg comes forward, slightly beyond front leg. Forward leg touches the ground at the knees.
6. Stand straight up, not forward bringing one leg up and out to the side.
7. Leg continues figure eight movement to the side and body leans opposite to follow.
8. Complete step and repeat.

How to Tell the Difference Between a Bionic Person and a Real Person

BIONIC PERSON

Can run 65 mph in slow motion with some one going "Di-di-di-di-di"

Can jump thirty feet up, over, or down

Can lift a refrigerator with one arm without scratching the floor

Can lift the back of a car off the ground so the bad guys can't get away

Can bend one-inch-thick steel

Can punch or kick through six inches of concrete

Can see 200 yards away with a 20:1 zoom as long as someone's going "Di-di-di-di-di"

Can hear a half mile away as long as the hair is pulled away from the ear

REAL PERSON

Can run 5 mph if he/she hasn't eaten any thing heavy

Can jump up and down, especially if angry

Can lift a refrigerator with the help of three friends and a lot of grunting

Can read the license plate of the bad guy's car if lucky

Can bend a clothes hanger back into shape

Can punch or kick six inches of concrete and hurt a toe

Can see a road sign 200 yards away but will have no idea what it means

Can hear the phone ring in the next room

How to Serve Tea to a Puma

Bugs Bunny: the King of Gamesmanship. He lures his opponents in and then moves in for the kill. He is the wise warrior who enters the fight head-on and attacks from every side. He is the hero who very few can take advantage of. He is the savior of little bunny rabbits who can't protect themselves from the ways of the world. Learn by doing:

1. Let a puma approach you dressed as Mrs. Bunny Rabbit, the little rabbit's mother.
2. Be courteous. You know it's a puma, but the puma doesn't know you know. Offer her a seat at your table. You could say,"Oh, well, Mrs. Rabbit, you must have some tea with me."
3. Show Mrs. Rabbit over to the table. At this point it would be wise to wink at the little rabbit so he knows you have not fallen for the puma's trick.
4. Pour Mrs. Rabbit a cup of tea and ask if she would like one lump or two. Hold up the sugar bowl.
5. It is a well-known fact that pumas do like sugar. "Why, yes," the puma will say.
6. Wait until the puma responds, "Oh, better make it three or four."
7. Now is your moment. Pull a club from underneath the table and beat the puma about the head with it three or four times. Do not jump the gun and, above all, give the puma only the requested number of lumps.

Hint: You can usually get away with this two or three times in a row before the puma catches on. But use your best judgement and, above all, have fun.

"Nice planet."
Worf, *Star Trek: The Next Generation*

"Whenever we think of dangerous claws, we usually think of the big cat family. But an anteater also has claws."
Marlin Perkins, *Mutual of Omaha's Wild Kingdom*

"I ain't got time to stand around here and discuss trivial trivialities."
Barney Fife, *The Andy Griffith Show*

Mr. F: Ciao!
Mork: Pekinese!
Mork and Mindy

"Hey, Splits! Let's Split!"
Bingo, *Banana Splits*

SUPER BONUS SECTION:
TV FANTASIES

We've all fantasized about our favorite TV shows at one point or another. I don't mean about what Jacqueline Smith would look like in a string bikini or what Tom Selleck looks like in a hot tub—I'm talking about fantasizing about the show itself—asking "What if?"

"What if Alice quit *The Brady Bunch?*" "What if we could read Captain Stubing's diary?" "What did Tattoo do after he left *Fantasy Island?*" These sorts of questions are the ones we'll answer here, in our bonus section on TV fantasies.

● ● ● ● ● ● ● ● ● ● ● ● ● ● ● ● ●

Alice Resigns: Lunchbox Notes to the Bradys

There are times in life when our daily routine becomes mundane and boring. There are times in television when our beloved characters and their lives begin to lose our interest. And usually in both cases, a change is called for. In the 70s, however, people didn't like change. People searched for status quo, and anything that changed within that was pushed aside. But now we have grown. We are ready for change. We are ready to face certain realities, like: What if Alice just gets totally fed up with the Bradys and decides to quit? As adults, we can face realities such as this one.

Dear Mike,

You and your scale model homes can go straight to Hell! I'm tired of picking up your scraps of cardboard, walking your damn dog, and being nanny to your brat pack of shallow, ugly twerps.

The perms you and your boys got suit you fine. You all look like the Brillo pads that you are. Consider this my resignation. Watch out for your mouthwash. I may have accidentally spiked it with Liquid Plumber.

Alice

Dear Carol,

You are the only one I really cared for. So that's why I tell you this: Mike and I have been having an affair for seven years now!

Sorry,

Alice

P.S. I'll have my friend call you about that new Wesson Oil product. He's interested to hear what you have to say.

Dear Greg,

If you think I don't know why you really moved up to the attic, you're dumber than your five-inch collars. I've got pictures, too. If you don't want anyone to see them, bring your allowance to Sam's every week. Put it in the lean ground beef and walk away. This is for me and all those girls whose hearts you squashed with your bell bottoms and that mop of hair.

Alice

Dear Marcia,

Get off your princess trip already. I'm glad you lost the school president election. With a head as big as yours it's no wonder it got hit by that football.

By the way, I do think you're fat. Slut.

Alice

Dear Peter,

You know, when you lost your job at the bike shop after working only one day, I felt really bad— really bad for your parents to have to look at your pathetic, sniveling, weasel face every day and know they were responsible for creating such a miserable failure of a man.

Good Luck,
Alice

Dear Jan,

I know you won the Ms. Popularity contest at school. And guess what, in my book you're #1. Number One Tramp! If you think you're going to grow up into some successful wife you've got another think coming, sister! You keep going the way you are and I'll lay you ten-to-one odds you wind up stripping in some sleazy Country bar. I'll see you in Hell!

Alice

Dear Bobby,

If ever there was a bigger momma's boy, I've never seen one. You and your whiny attitude can go cry- ing right back to Mom. You remember that baloney sandwich I made you the day Tiger disappeared? Well, that wasn't baloney. And Tiger ain't coming back, Bright Boy!

Alice

Dear Cindy,

Two words to you, Candy Queen: Thpeech Therapy! Live it, love it, be it.

Alice

Tattoola

Hervé Villachaise is dead, of course. But what if he weren't? What if he followed in the footsteps of Jim Nabors and Adrian Zmed and followed his dream to sing on stage? In fact, in a parallel universe, his evil twin is performing in Las Vegas with a bad goatee.

Here are the lyrics to one of his medley tunes to be sung to the tune of "Lola" by the Kinks.

I applied for a job
Down in Wai Ki-Ki
Where you pay lots of money for a fantasy
On an Island
I-I-I-I-Island

I looked for a man
Who was in a white suit
He look at me and he noticed I was cute
Oh, my Boss
B-B-B-B-Boss

I watch all day
And I watch all night
For the coming of that fantastic flight
Oh, de plane
D-D-D-Dee plane!

The Boss he worries,
And he ain't no dork
Wants the guests to have fun
He's called Mr. Roarke
Mr. Roarke
Mr.—I don't know—Ro-arke!

Bridge:
Oh I'm not the world's most tallest man
I see your eyes as best I can
My Boss doesn't mind, so neither should you
But if you do, I'll stomp on your shoe

Oh, Tattoola
Tat-Tat-Tat-Tattoola
Tat-Tat-Tat-Tattoola
Tat-Tat-Tat-Tattoola

Regal Beagle Blue Plate Specials

Monday—Chrissy's Brains and Eggs
Tuesday—Jack's Manly Steak and Potatoes
Wednesday—Mr. Roper's Salt Peter Pasta
Thursday—Mrs. Roper's Only Chocolate Delight
Friday—Janet's Dateless Surprise
Saturday—Larry's Crabs
Sunday—Misunderstood Meatloaf (two for the price of three)

Al's Blue Plate Specials

Monday—Ralph Malph's Tongue Sandwich
Tuesday—Potsie's Pot Roast
Wednesday—Richie's Cunning-Ham Sandwich
Thursday—Jenny's Pickle-O
Friday—Fonzie's Cool Cucumber Sandwich
Saturday—Joanie's Chachi'-in-a-Blanket
Sunday—Chachi's Joanies-on-a-Roll

Cheers Blue Plate Appetizers

Monday—Diane's Pompous Pesto
Tuesday—Woodie's Hanover Hog's Hocks
Wednesday—Carla's Seven Husband Stew
Thursday—Frasier's Cold Wife Lasagna
Friday—Sam's Tail (Maine Lobster)
Saturday—Cliff's Lame Duck
Sunday—Norm's Beer Nuts

Beverly Hillbillies 90210

Coincidence? Is *Beverly Hills 90210* character driven or plot driven? Is *The Beverly Hillbillies* everyone's fantasy life? Or vice-versa? However you think, the two shows, though nearly twenty years apart, are much closer than they seem at first glance. This is why we think *90210* is a spin-off of *The Beverly Hillbillies*.

The Clampitts moved from Oklahoma to Beverly Hills.	The Walshes moved from Minnesota to Beverly Hills.
Jethro Clampitt drives a Model T.	Brandon Walsh drives an old Mustang.
Jed Clampitt has no business sense, yet is a multi-millionaire.	Jim Walsh has no sense, yet is a multi-millionaire.
Granny Clampitt is as stubborn as a mule.	Donna looks like a mule.
Ellie May is a "simple" blonde, wanting to find a husband.	Kelly is a thin-nosed blonde, wanting to find some husbands.
Mr. Drysdale kisses Clampitt ass.	David is an ass.
Ms. Hathaway is a feminist.	Andrea tries to be feminine.

Coincidence? The similarities are spellbinding. But you decide.

Schneider's To Do List

- [ ] Fix toilet in 4C.
- [ ] Fix Ms Romano's sink again.
- [ ] Shellac the front door.
- [ ] Proposition Ms. Romano.
- [ ] Deal with her rejection.
- [ ] Paint bannisters.
- [ ] Introduce Barbara to the nice Van Halen boy in 3A.
- [ ] Fix door in 3D.
- [ ] Compliment Julie—Tell her how much she lookslike that singer from the Mamas and Papas.
- [ ] Proposition Ms. Romano again.
- [ ] Give lots of advice that no one listens to.

The Brady Bunch à la Quentin Tarantino

It was in 1969 that we were first introduced to the family values of the Brady family. In such a large family that came from two different worlds (one was a lovely lady, the other was a man named Brady), it was surprising that for the five-year run of the show, the only fights were over things as simple as bathroom time, and who got to move into the attic.

But what if the Brady household was not always such a calm place? What if tensions over the years had continued to grow and the Brady family worked out their problems in a 90s fashion rather than over brownies and milk? Here's what we think Quentin Tarantino would have made of the Bradys—this is much more than a hunch.

Int. Clubhouse—Morning

An average American backyard hand-built clubhouse in the Brady yard. It's about 8:30 A.M. The place is filthy: It's a sloppy boy's club. Sitting in a circle around a makeshift table are Greg, Peter, and Bobby. They are all smoking cigarettes like it's the end of the world.

BOBBY: Why don't we just let those dumb girls in here . . . I mean, I don't like 'em either, but—

PETER: You always give in first, Bobby. . . . Don't be such a pus! Just give 'em what they want!

GREG: Common! Both of 'ya. We gotta work together on this. . . . If we give those f*cking girls a share of our clubhouse, it's as f*cking bad as handin' them our f*cking lives and sayin', 'Okay, stupid girls, whatever you want.' We gotta bring a f*cking end to this tonight. I'm tired of putting up with their sh*t.

Both Bobby and Peter nod their heads. Alice peeks her head through the sheet covering the door.

ALICE: You boys need some more juice?

PETER: No thanks, I'm fine.

BOBBY: I could use some more coffee.

Alice laughs and throws him a 'Oh, you card' look. Bobby pulls his gun and shoots her right between her eyes. Bobby lights up another cigarette.

GREG: I'm telling you, I'm callin' an end to this truce. I am the f*ckin' gatekeeper here and those chicks are the f*ckin' straws that broke the camel's back. This is it, it's tonight or never.

Marcia, Jan, and Cindy come barging in the door. All three are dressed to kill. All three stand smiling with their hands behind their backs.

MARCIA: We've come to clear the air.

PETER: Well then you creeps better leave 'cause you're stinkin' up the place.

JAN: You got Alice, huh? I never liked her lunches anyway . . . but hey you guys, enough is enough.

CINDY: Yea, what thee thaid.

BOBBY: Okay thindy . . . you thniveling thnake!

MARCIA: Shake?

All three girls bring their hands forward, all wielding small caliber handguns. But Greg, Peter, and Bobby aren't slow. They see it coming and pull their guns. The sounds of cocking hammers and safety releases can be heard. Everyone either has a gun trained on them, or is trained at someone. Either way, it's tense.

GREG: Okay, let's not be like Jack Tripper and start gettin' clumsy.

MARCIA: Either we're staying here all day with our guns, or we all gonna die.

Cindy starts to cry and lowers her gun.

CINDY: I can't take thith anymore you guyth. We're all the thame blood here.

The rest start to look at each other and slowly lower their guns. Bobby gets up to comfort Cindy. He puts his arm around her. Cindy, still crying, pulls Bobby's head back by the hair and blows his brains out. As he's falling, she grabs his gun and shoots Greg and Peter.

MARCIA: Nice move Cindy, we can always count on you.

Cindy, dripping with blood and brains, pulls her guns and shoots Marcia and Jan. All is quiet. Just then, Carol and Mike come bursting in.

MIKE: What the heck happened here?

CINDY (*crying*): They wanted me to share my clubhouse.

She shoots and kills Mike and Carol.

We pull away from Cindy in the clubhouse, a bloody cesspool. She walks in circles around the bodies and hums Duane Eddy's "Rebel Rouser."

Fade to black.

Mr. Roarke's Diary

Mr. Roarke was a complex and tortured man. By his own choice, he devoted his life to fulfilling other people's fantasies, all on beautiful *Fantasy Island*. His only friend was Tattoo. But they rarely spoke; they didn't really see eye to eye.

Fantasy Island: April 18, 1981

Business as usual on the island again today. Plane came, Tattoo rang bell, yelled "Dee plane! Dee plane!" again. Why must he insist on doing that every week? It's not as if we don't know when to expect the dear guests—they arrive the same time every week.

I'm a little worried about Mrs. Lydia Daniels. Her great great great great grandmother was a member of the French aristocracy, and she wants to experience life as her grandmother did. Those were difficult times, especially for a woman. She may come back with a greater understanding of history, and of who she is—or, she may not come back at all. . . .

Whatever. I've already deposited her check.

I think the tropics are finally starting to affect my judgement. I keep thinking I recognize my guests from popular TV shows. I could have sworn that a few weeks ago Florence Henderson was here—and just last week, a Robert Reed look-alike was visiting. They were both going by different names, but the resemblance was uncanny.

Question: Are white suits passé?

My Fantasies

To own a Volare, with that rich, Corinthian leather
To meet Jaqueline Smith or Kate Jackson
To go somewhere where I can just relax and have others attend to me—*The Love Boat?*

Captain's Log: THE LOVE BOAT

Captain Stubing was a tough nut to crack. Distinguished, even in those shorts, Merrill ran a clean ship, and always knew what advice to give his passengers and crew to make them feel welcome. He obviously had a past, and feelings too—but he rarely showed them, even to his close friend, Doc. Now, on the 10th anniversary of *The Love Boat*'s last cruise (1986), we finally gain a glimpse into what made Merrill Stubing tick. Archivists at Spelling Entertainment have released previously unpublished captain's logs from *The Love Boat*'s many trips. This is the first time any of these logs has appeared in print.

SEA DATE: JANUARY 5, 1982

Day One: Left Los Angeles on time again. Big fanfare, as usual. The passengers seem happy—particularly the fiery Spanish vixen who came aboard today. Her name is April, and she set my sea-weary heart aflame. When I saw her come aboard I could feel my bald head turning red underneath my hat. The Cunninghams came aboard again as well. They look very happy.

Day Two: Seas are calm—in fact, as long as I can remember, we've never had a stormy voyage. You'd think after all these years of cruising, we'd at least run into a tropical storm or two—but no, nothing. I'm a little worried about Julie—she disappears frequently into the bathroom on the Promenade Deck, and comes back glossy eyed and sniffing. She must be very upset about something. I hope she's okay. The Cunninghams looked a little tense at the Captain's table today.

Day Three: Doc introduced me to another one of his ex-wives again. I think this is the ninth one I've met. He's got more exes than Elizabeth Taylor (who happened to be on the ship last week!). The Cunninghams were fighting today over the shuffleboard. I'm a little concerned.

Day Four: Julie disappeared into the bathroom again during dinner tonight and reappeared sniffing. Something's really getting to her. Mr. Cunningham is spending a lot of time alone on the Fiesta Deck. I think I'll go talk to him after dinner and see what's what.

Day Five: Gopher averted a near catastrophe on the Lido Deck today with Mr. and Mrs. Hartley—it seems that they were perfectly happy when they came aboard, but were having a few difficulties midway through the cruise. A lot of our passengers seem to experience the same pattern. Must be that most people aren't used to the sea air. Anyway, Gopher had a talk with both of them, and fifteen minutes later, they were in each other's arms, just like newlyweds. He never ceases to amaze me—his diplomatic skills are astounding. He might make a good congressman someday if he weren't only a ship's burser. Had a fine talk myself with Mr. Cunningham last night. Hope he resolves things.

Day Six: If Vicki calls me "Captain Merrill" one more time, she's going over. Mr. and Mrs. Cunningham were holding hands today by the pool.

Day Seven: Isaac is so fast! How can he be in the Pirate's Cove in one second, by the pool in another, and on the Promenade Deck the next? He's outtasight!

Day Eight: We arrived back in Los Angeles on time again. All passengers in love and accounted for. How do we do it?

The M*A*S*H 4077th

We may have all seen each episode of *M*A*S*H* three or four times. And why not? It ran from 1972–1983 and continues to air at least twice a day in most cities around America. Sure, there is the random episode that doesn't strike a familiar chord until about halfway through, but for the most part *M*A*S*H* was like Archie comics to the collector: You knew the story and the jokes after looking at the first few frames.

There is, however, one aspect to *M*A*S*H* that continues to confuse us occasionally. Where is the women's shower in relation to the Swamp? Where exactly is the basketball hoop, and Rosie's Bar? Well, after weeks of intensive research and careful study, we have prepared a map to help you find your way around the 4077th—Best Care Anywhere.

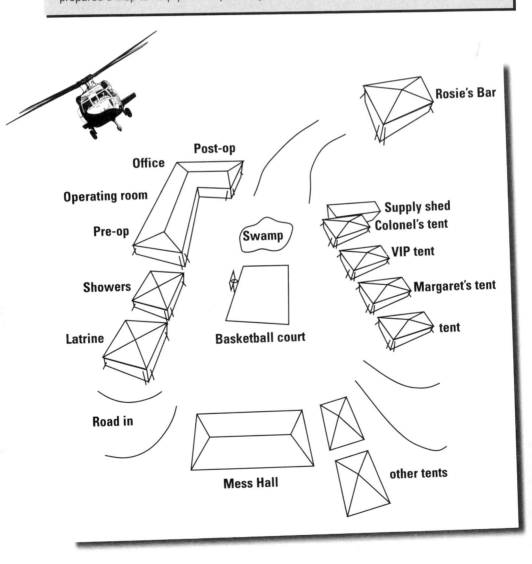

Map of the Islands (Gilligan's, Fantasy, Land of the Lost)

Did you ever wonder if the *Love Boat* ever docked at *Fantasy Island?* Or if Gilligan ever stumbled upon a bottomless pit that led to the *Land of the Lost?* Did you wonder if maybe, just maybe, if the *Love Boat* had taken a different course for their Japanese cruise, they would have seen the signal fire that the professor built, and Gilligan and Mary Anne would have hooked up on the Lido Deck on the way back to L.A.?

Well, here is a map to show you the likelihood of all that happening, from a geographical point of view. Not to scale. Not to exact longitudinal coordinates. But with our best guesstimates of the location of *Gilligan's Island, Fantasy Island,* the *Land of the Lost,* and the *Love Boat's* stops along its way.

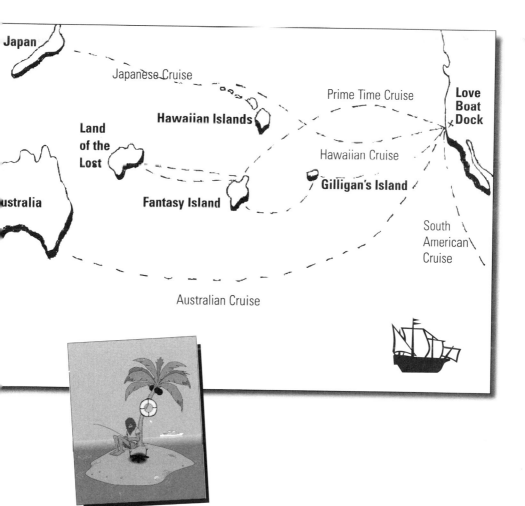

GOOD NIGHT, JOHNBOY:
EXITS AND CLOSING WORDS

In courtly days, the process of taking one's leave was a ritual of respect. Subjects would not turn their backs on the nobility—they would profess their love and admiration, their undying loyalty, then bow and exit. This process implied a mutual respect; it showed that the subjects honored their rulers enough to give them words of security in their absence and, in turn, that the nobles valued their friendship enough to give them humble blessings.

Even on TV saying goodbye was always a ritual. Sometimes our TV friends would trust us to come back to them next week and simply say a *Sesame Street* "See ya." Sometimes they were afraid we wouldn't return, so they'd give us a Batman-esque cliffhanger to draw us back to next week's program.

Either way, it was goodbye. As you read through this collection of those memorable adieus, know that we leave you as well. We bow, profess our undying loyalty, and say farewell.

● ● ● ● ● ● ● ● ● ● ● ● ● ● ● ●

"Aloha, suckers!"
Steve McGarrett, *Hawaii Five-0*

"We'll be back in two and two."
Chuck Woolery, *The Love Connection*

"Exit, stage left."
Snagglepuss, *Snagglepuss*

"Did I tell you what happened last week to my Aunt Esther . . . Last week Aunt Esther was sitting in her living room when the doorbell rang. She answered the door and there was a nice young man there who says, 'I have a telegram for you.' She says, 'You know what I've wanted my whole life? A singing telegram.' He says, 'Lady this is not a singing telegram.' She says, 'Would you begrudge an old lady a singing telegram?' He says, 'Alright lady.' He opens it up and goes, 'Da-da-da-da-da, your sister Rose is dead. It seems that she died in bed.'"
Gabe Kotter, *Welcome Back, Kotter*

"Don't take the law into your own hands . . . take 'em to court."
Doug Lewellyn, *The People's Court*

Be with us next time for 'A Leak in the Lake' or 'The Drainmaker.'
Rocky and Bullwinkle

"Don't miss the next thrill-packed episode in *The Adventures of Superman.*"
Announcer, *The Adventures of Superman*

"Th-th-th, th-th-th, th-th-that's all, folks!"
Porky Pig, *Looney Tunes*

"Adios am-i-gos!"
Huckleberry Hound, *Huckleberry Hound*

"'Til next week! Nanu nanu!"
Mork, *Mork and Mindy*

"Let us depart! We've nary an excess moment."
Henchman, *Batman*

Fleeing from the Cylon tyranny, the last Battlestar Galactica leads a ragtag, fugitive fleet, on a lonely quest for a shining planet known as Earth.
Battlestar Galactica

"Your fantasy is over."
Mr. Roarke, *Fantasy Island*

"Find out tomorrow. Same Bat Time. Same Bat Channel."
Batman

It's such a good feeling
To know you're alive.
It's such a happy feeling,
You're growing inside.
And when you wake up ready to say,
"I'm gonna make a snappy new day."
It's such a good feeling,
A very good feeling,
A feeling you know . . .
That I'll be back,
When the week is new
And I'll have more
Ideas for you
And you'll have things
You'll want to talk about
I will too!
Mister Rogers, *Mr. Rogers' Neighborhood*

"Sesame Street has been brought to you today by the letters *J* and *M*. And by the number *5*. Sesame Street is a production of the Children's Television Workshop."
Sesame Street

"Good night, John-boy."
Everyone, *The Waltons*

Five Great Rod Serling Speeches from
TWILIGHT ZONE

From 1959 to 1964, television audiences were introduced to a "fifth dimension, beyond that which is known to man." It was a dimension of sight, sound, mind, and of narrators with tightly clenched teeth. Some of television and moviedom's greatest stars got their starts on *The Twilight Zone,* including Roddy McDowell, Jack Warden, Robert Redford, and William Shatner. The episodes were marked for their black humor, their high quality scripts, and by the trademark Serling narrations that opened each show. Here are five of Serling's best monologues.

For the record, prejudices can kill and suspicion can destroy, and a thoughtless, frightened search for a scapegoat has a fallout of its own—for the children, and the children yet unborn. And the pity of it is that these things cannot be confined—to *The Twilight Zone.*

Just how normal are we? Just who are the people we nod our hellos to as we pass on the street? A rather good question to ask—particularly in *The Twilight Zone.*

All persons attempting to conceal criminal acts involving their cars are hereby warned: Check first to see that underneath that chrome there does not lie a conscience, especially if you're driving along a rain-soaked highway—in *The Twilight Zone.*

We know that a dream can be real, but who ever thought that reality could be a dream? We exist, of course, but how, in what way? Are we flesh-and-blood human beings, or are we simply part of someone's feverish, complicated nightmare? Think about it, and then ask yourself, Do you live here, in this country, in this world, or do you live instead—in *The Twilight Zone?*

The subject: fear. The cure: a little more faith. A Rx off the shelf—in *The Twilight Zone.*

The Final Showcase
from THE PRICE IS RIGHT

It is a well-known fact that more merchandise has been given away on this game show than on any other. On the air in one form or another since 1956, *The Price Is Right* is essentially about how well consumers know what they're consuming—basically, it's one big ad.

Of course, the best part of the show is Bob Barker presenting the "showcase showdown," the best of which are planned around a theme. Some of these are fairly straightforward—others reach into the realm of the ridiculous. The ridiculous is what you'll find below. Here are seven actual showcases, and their ridiculous premises.

☐ The Big John, Roving Reporter Showcase—Johnny Olson, the announcer, played a man-in-the-street reporter who asked questions that related to the prizes.

☐ The Fabulous Moving Company Showcase—Holly and Kathleen, in gold jumpsuits, delivered, well, fabulous prizes.

☐ The Flakey Flick Showcase—Prizes were introduced in the guise of film parodies, which included "King Solomon's Wines," "Socky," and "Hercules Unstrung."

☐ The Godmother Showcase—Janice played a mobstress, offering prizes you couldn't refuse.

☐ The Obi-Wan Kniblick Showcase—Johnny plays a mountain guru and the girls climb the mountain in turn to have their fortunes read.

☐ The Rappin' Rod Showcase—Johnny plays a rap star, and Holly and Kathleen play his fly girls.

☐ Nursery Showcase—The models played babies.

INDEX

ABOUT THE
AUTHORS

That's David on the left, Joe on the right.

David Borgenicht is a writer and editor who does a really good Mr. Roarke impression. He has edited several books of quotations, is the author of several children's books, and has written for many publications, including *Philadelphia* magazine. He grew up in Salt Lake City, Utah, where he and his brother Joe spent entirely too much time watching TV and memorizing the lines. (Their parents told them they couldn't watch as much TV as they did, but they didn't listen. As a result, they became obsessed. The pay-off came when they had to do the the research for this book—they were tortured by having to watch all the shows over and over again. Ah, revenge is a TV dinner served cold.) David currently lives in Philadelphia with his wife, Suzanne, and their surround sound TV system.

Joe Quijote Borgenicht is a truck driver from Salt Lake City, Utah. He graduated, despite his best efforts, from a small college in Brunswick, Maine, where it was' too damn cold to do anything but turn on the heat and the cable. Most of his young and adult education included watching *Three's Company* while practicing speling, watching *The Bugs Bunny/Road Runner Show* and *Rocky and Bullwinkle,* while studying math. He's smarter than he looks, and dumber than he feels. But he's working on it.

Any collection of quotes and wisdom is bound to leave a few empty spaces. But dammit, we're trying to fill them. We're already hard at work collecting quotations and sidebars for the next anthology—quotes from both TV and movies. E-mail us your favorites. Anyone who submits a quote we use will receive a hearty "thank you" in the next acknowledgments section. What a deal, huh? Send your submissions to DavidABorg@aol.com. The world will thank you.